A TEEN'S GUIDE TO
WELLNESS, PURPOSE & ABUNDANCE

PATTY MCLAIN M.ED.

Young Living™ and *Young Living*™ *Essential Oils* are registered trademarks of *Young Living Essential Oils, LLC.*

The views presented in this book are those of the author and do not necessarily represent the views of *Young Living*™. *A Teen's Guide to Wellness, Purpose, and Abundance* is not sponsored or endorsed by *Young Living*™ or by D. Gary & Mary Young. The FDA has not evaluated any statements and suggestions or products discussed are not intended to treat, diagnose, or cure any disease.

Visit us at: www.thepattymclain.com

Book Cover Design by Kristy Jamison

ISBN-10: 1545128782
ISBN-13: 978-545128787

DEDICATION

This book is dedicated to all my kids past, present and future. I am so blessed to work with teens and young adults and I know that I have learned more from you than I could ever possibly teach. Thank you for reminding me that I need to practice what I preach and for inspiring me to get out of my comfort zone and out of my own way.

Contents

ACKNOWLEDGMENTS

I know I wouldn't be here or have this stellar opportunity if I didn't have the most amazing people in my life. My infinite love and gratitude belongs to:

My husband, Jason "Bird" McLain, for his love, encouragement, and support in every way since we were teens.

Our son, Ian, for inspiring me to be more present, to play every day, and to learn how to take care of myself and embrace wellness so I can take care of him and be my best self.

My Aunt Linda for being a wellness warrior, for encouraging me to embark on this journey, and for her tireless work editing and formatting the manuscript.

My Mom, Dad, and entire family for putting up with me when I was a teen and pushing me to leverage my strengths to help others.

Jessica Hellman, Robin Boynosky, Erica Rafter, Robin Kiesinger, Angela Kiesinger, Brandi Woodward, George Benjamin, Jenna Maus-Colucci and Lori Tasci for sticking with me since WE were teens, for always knowing exactly when there is a disruption in the force, and for navigating the entire wellness spectrum with me.

Doug Womelsdorf for his infinite and unconditional love, support, resources and acceptance.

Bella Cox and the teens in my wellness workshops along with the other important young people in my life - Tim and Sean Smith, Calvin Craig, Autumn and Kaelyn Legg, and Siera Hall - for discussing these concepts with me and piloting many of the prompts and activities.

Nora Riley and our entire Pathways family for teaching me so many of the lessons in this guide and for their unconditional love, support and encouragement.

Melissa Russo, Meghan Feliciani, Kimberly Maslanka, Amy Lapp, Terra McAulliffe, my awesome Empowered by Nature team, the NEPA Oilers community, and my amazing sideline sisters Kristen O'Connell and Stephanie VanNostrand for being there every step of the way and for teaching me about wellness, purpose, and abundance so that I can pay it forward.

The entire Young Living community, especially D. Gary and Mary Young for being visionaries, pioneers and brilliant, heart-centered leaders, my upline leaders, Kathy Kouwe and Connie Marie McDanel for showing me what is possible, the Oola Guys Dr. Troy and Dr. Dave for encouraging me to share Oola with teens, Dr. Ben Perkus for giving me AFT as a tool to get through all of the emotional barriers that were stopping me from finishing this book, Sarah Harnish for giving my team a *Gameplan*, Steve Sheridan for teaching me about financial wellness, Monique McLean for giving me my first experience with prayer, and Adam Green for proving that young people can do big things.

HeathCliff Rothman for including me with Everyone Matters.

My Pleasant Valley family for always being there for me and encouraging me to follow my dreams.

All of my teachers, especially Tomm Evans and Dr. Agnes Cardoni, who told me a very long time ago that I could write and that I could make a difference.

Last but not least, I want to thank whomever formulated Ningxia Nitro™ and the person who invented group text messages ☺

Hi There!

Before we get started, I want you to know that I did not write this to tell you what to do or who to be - I want you to be YOU.

I wrote this guide as a resource because you are amazing and you have choices. I also wrote this to help you become aware of some of the toxins that affect all of us on different levels and to make sure you're equally aware of all of the positive things impacting your life. Awareness is the first step toward creating positive experiences and my goal is to help you have as many amazing experiences as possible.

Another thing I want you to know is that I'm a real person, just like you. I am not a guru and, as you'll read, there are some topics I cover in this guide that I'm still learning about myself. I actually have a little note in this section to write something heart-centered and really connect with you as my reader, but then I totally over-thought that and decided that it'll be easier for you to just see me as real. I am perfectly imperfect, but I am passionate about sharing these ideas with you in an open-ended and interactive way, so I'm really glad you're here. In honor of my imperfections, you might even encounter a typo along the way, but the teacher in me will tell you that they are in there on purpose to make sure that you're paying attention.

This guide has evolved a few times. Initially, my plan was to focus completely on essential oils because I know how much they help with wellness mentally, emotionally, spiritually, and physically. As I began writing and constructing the outline, things shifted because, as you will learn, wellness is a lifestyle and essential oils are a lot more effective when they are used as part of that bigger context of wellness. So, you're going to learn a lot about Young Living™ because this is still an essential oil guide, but it is also a guide to overall wellness, empowerment, self-love and connection.

I'm not sure if you're here because of a well-meaning adult in your life or because you are already passionate about wellness, purpose, and abundance, but my goal is to offer you some hope, tools, and inspiration.

Honestly, if you've opened the guide and gotten this far, you've already done half the work. By the time you are finished exploring, I hope you will have enough tips, tricks, and incentive to fully embrace your awesomeness by making the best choices for your body, mind, and spirit.

Since there seems to be a tremendous focus on all of the things young people CAN'T do, this guide is going to take things from a slightly different angle as it focuses on some things that you CAN do while providing plenty of resources to support you as you continue to dream big and be your best self!

My intention is to give you plenty of outlets to shine, share your dreams, and inspire others, so I'm starting with a brand-new Instagram account @Teen_Oiler. I also plan to create a presence on YouTube, SnapChat, and whatever other fun platforms pop up while I'm on this adventure, but I am definitely going to need some help from YOU to keep the content interesting, fun, and relevant. As you'll see, there are plenty of opportunities for you to share your thoughts and ideas throughout the guide, so I've also included space for you to brainstorm some social media connections so you can infuse the Internet with a little more positivity and wellness!

Last, but not least, I am not a medical professional or a mental health professional. I am an Independent Distributor of Young Living. The information in this book is not meant to diagnose, treat, cure, or prevent any disease. The information represents what I, an Independent Distributor of Young Living essential oils, have chosen to do to take charge of my wellness. Statements in this guide have not been evaluated by the Food and Drug Administration. If you are pregnant, nursing, taking medication, or have a medical condition, consult your physician before using any products.

Information found in this book is meant for educational and informational purposes only and to inspire you to make your own wellness decisions based on your own research and in partnership with your healthcare provider.

GETTING THE MOST OUT OF THIS GUIDE

Now that we have all of that out of the way, there are a few other things I would like you to keep in mind before you begin reading:

- You are a unique individual and so is everyone else, so that means there is no magic bullet, one-size-fits-all approach to wellness.
- Keep an open mind.
- Avoid the comparison trap and self-judgment as much as possible.
- Remember that there is no right or wrong way to empower yourself – the tips and stories that I share are just a place to start your journey.
- Give yourself permission to explore each concept at least once.
- Take what works for you and leave the rest.
- This guide is not a compilation of everything I know about teens or about wellness because that would be a little too intense.
- My goal is to give you a little information on a lot of topics. I am planting the seeds, but it is up to you to water them.
- This guide is an opportunity for you to start thinking about some important topics so you can better understand how you think, feel, and interact with the world.
- In many ways, the thoughts that you pour into these pages are even more important than the ones that I will provide for you, so USE the guide. Write in it. Color it. Add your –ness to it and own it.
- If you are reading this guide on a Kindle or other digital e-reader, you're going to need a notebook for your thoughts, feelings, colors, and doodles.
- You do not need ALL of the resources and essential oils that are suggested throughout the book and you can still get a lot out of this book if you aren't an oiler. Hopefully you'll be inspired to kick a few toxins out of your life, and if you are, be sure to connect with the person that recommended this book to you so they can teach you more and help you on your path to wellness, purpose, and abundance.

- I included plenty of different ways to approach each topic. If social media isn't your thing, skip that part. If you're not sure about essential oils just yet, try some lavender before bed for a few nights. If you get stuck in one part, move on and come back to it later.
- There is no right or wrong way to do this.
- Have fun!

WELCOME

This guide is about helping you understand and explore choices and connections because, at the end of the day, connections keep us going and choices are what guide the way. We can have all of the tips and tools in the world, but if we feel disconnected and don't take ownership of our choices, we can still end up in toxic situations.

In honor of the connections we are going to create in this guide, I want to share a little bit more about me and my story so you know where I'm coming from and I also want you to start thinking about who YOU are and what kind of choices you're already making.

A LITTLE BIT ABOUT ME...

There are a few things you might need to know before we begin. At the very least, there are a few things that make me uniquely qualified for this adventure.

FIRST OF ALL, I AM YOUR BIGGEST FAN. I know I might not know you (yet), but I believe in you. I believe that each and every individual on this planet is amazingly equipped with unique gifts and talents, along with limitless capacity for love – including you. How could I not be your biggest fan when you have all of THAT going on?

I AM NOT A DOCTOR OR AN "EXPERT" OR ANYONE THAT IS GOING TO CLAIM TO "FIX" YOU. My main goal is to help you see all of the parts of you that are indestructible and limitless so you know, without a doubt, you can't be "broken." I do have a lot of experience and a bunch of degrees. Basically, the experience and degrees make me look qualified to other adults but, at the end of the day, I'm a lot like you. I get excited. I get frustrated. I succeed. I fail. I make really good choices and I make really bad choices, but I always learn a LOT. This guide is my first attempt at sharing a little bit about some of the most important things I've learned along the way in the hope that you will connect with them and maybe even pass them on to someone else that you care about.

I AM NOT A TEENAGER... but I was one and I've devoted my life to working with and empowering teens because I have seen the amazing potential that exists when young people practice some of the things we will explore in this guide.

As a teen, I was full of quirks and insecurities. Actually I was probably equal parts quirky, insecure, nerdy, and fun (although I'm sure my parents would have a different equation that also involved me being sarcastic and lazy). I liked to listen to all kinds of music and read all kinds of books, I liked to experiment with fashion, I loved my friends more than anything, and I even spent a good chunk of my junior year of high school carrying around the original Tickle Me Elmo.

As a teen, I also had absolutely no clue about wellness. My weight fluctuated as wildly as my hair color, everyone in my family smoked, and I lived on cereal, ice pops, and my mom's amazing down-home southern cooking.

Thanks to some stress and anxiety from a failed relationship and related struggles with my squad my Senior year, I did manage to lose a lot of weight, but it wasn't because I was working out or eating nutritious food - it was 100% stress related. It turns out that skinny doesn't always mean healthy... who knew?

I found all of the weight I had lost, and then some, when I started college, and I also found a lot more stress. Since no one ever told me how to cope with challenges or deal with stress, and since I tended to be an over-achieving, people pleasing, perfectionist, my stress and anxiety just kept getting worse and worse.

Then in my 20s, when my fiancé was diagnosed with Stage 4 cancer, my brother was killed by a drunk driver, and my work mentor and close friend died suddenly, I really started to lose it. I made bad choices with food and alcohol and most of the time, I felt like I couldn't breathe.

Thankfully I caught a break when I became a mom to Ian, my adorable little boy, but it also gave me a LOT to think about and a mission to find some tools to conquer my demons and get healthy – for his sake.

Ian was the initial catalyst for my journey into wellness, purpose, and abundance but teenagers ultimately became my best teachers as well as my best students as I learned about choices, mindset, and healthy living. They have all given me HOPE and that is what I intend to give to each and every one of you.

That brings us to the last thing that you need to know about me - HOPE is always my focus.

HOPE IS MY "WHY". As I mentioned earlier, I am not a psychologist or a well-documented expert, but I am a teacher and a parent and I have found my purpose in my passion for supporting young people in ways that allow their gifts and potential to shine. My life, so far, has been equal parts amazing and tragic but I now know that it was all perfectly leading me to the place where I am now so that I can bring HOPE to others in bigger and bigger ways

For every tragedy and trauma in my life, there has been a blessing, and I offer you the gift of this perspective so that you may have the courage to embrace your vulnerability, find your own blessings, and ultimately have HOPE.

I am paying forward the HOPE that my parents gave me, by giving my son even more opportunities and I am paying forward the HOPE that my teachers gave me, by connecting with you and introducing you to the tools and natural wellness that I wish I'd had back then. I'm also paying forward the HOPE, love and unconditional support that my entrepreneurial friends and mentors gave me by showing everyone I know and those I encounter that they have options and it is possible to get by on a HOPE and a dream because THAT faith moves mountains and is a catalyst for everything we can ever imagine and so much more!

A Little Bit about Young Living™...

Throughout this guide you are going to see many references to Young Living and Young Living Essential Oils because the company, the products and the amazing community inspired this whole project. Without my oils I never would've had the courage or the focus to tackle this, and without the amazing people in the Young Living community, I never could've had the confidence to share my work in such a big way.

Some would say that Young Living is just an essential oil company, but I know it is so much more and I am excited to share my understanding of this movement that is changing lives in infinite ways on every continent.

This book is not sponsored by or endorsed by Young Living and the thoughts are all mine, but it is my hope that you fall in love with this movement as much as I have because it epitomizes the wellness, purpose, and abundance we are about to explore together. I especially hope that you can see all of the opportunities for teens that I outlined in a recent blog post for the adults that love and care about you. We are going to dive deeper into all of this throughout the book, but this is a great place to start! Check out the blog and circle some of the reasons that are most interesting to you:

10 Reasons to Embrace Natural Wellness with Young Living

It's never been easy to be a teen, but things are getting more and more complicated in our globalized 21st century world. Young people are being labeled, judged, and challenged in new ways every day. Without good tools, guidance, and support, many of them struggle with a variety of obstacles like apathy, substance abuse, addiction, self-harm, and bullying to name just a few. However, the opposite is also true - with the right tools, guidance, and support, teens can thrive, innovate, and inspire positive changes in our world.

After working with teens and young adults for my entire career, I have many tools to share with them, but I am especially passionate about empowering them with natural wellness. When teens feel good and practice wellness, it is a lot easier to help them discover their purpose and give them other tools and opportunities for success.

When young people feel connected, understand a bigger picture and realize that they have choices; they can have an incredible impact on each other and the world around them. The Young Living lifestyle, products, company, and community can empower teens in so many crucial ways, but here are ten of my favorites!

With Young Living, teenagers can

1. Reduce Stress

I haven't met many teens (or people) that haven't struggled with stress from time to time. On those rough days, they can use essential oils like lavender and frankincense or blends like Stress Away™ and Peace and Calming™ to relax, rest, and renew. Good sleep, proper nutrition, and self care are all great ways to reduce stress and Young Living oils, supplements, and personal care products are the purest and most potent natural products on the market.

2. Support Wellness

Many teens feel indestructible in their good health and overall wellness while others suffer from the effects of poor nutrition, environmental toxins, and restless sleep. Young Living teaches everyone about the importance of proactive wellness and good choices. When teens take care of their bodies regularly with good nutrition, quality sleep, and toxin-free choices, their immune systems are fully supported along with all of the systems of the body so their bodies can do what they were designed to do and the focus can stay on wellness! Teens can use Thieves™ oil and the entire line of Thieves™ products and great supplements like Master Formula™, Life 9™, and Super C™ along with the nutrient infused Ningxia™ drinks to make sure they always feel great and have energy.

3. ALLEVIATE ODORS

From sneakers and gym bags to lockers and messy cars, there are often many unpleasant odors that can be alleviated with essential oils. Unfortunately, many people choose to cover up these smells with toxic sprays and other synthetic alternatives like scented candles that may end up creating more health problems. There are many essential oils that smell really good including lemon, lavender, peppermint, and orange, but my go-to oil to diffuse for bad odors is Purification™ and it also works in the vacuum, in sneakers and in the car vents!

4. DITCH TOXINS

Many young people have no clue what harmful toxins they put in and on their body every day. Thankfully, Young Living has a complete line of personal care products including shampoo, conditioner, face wash, body wash, lotions, massage oil, deodorant, toothpaste, and more! The Think Dirty app is my favorite way to analyze the lotions, hair products, and other personal care items that can cause serious long-term health issues. Download it now, scan some of your favorite items from the drug store and leave me a comment with the results – I have a feeling you'll be shocked at the ingredients!

5. CREATE CONNECTION

In order for teens to make good choices, it is important for them to feel connected to themselves, other people and to something bigger than themselves. The Young Living community fosters connection to the self by bringing awareness to thoughts, feelings, and physical wellness and there is also a very clear connection to a bigger picture that allows young people to explore their relationship to the Earth and to better understand their faith. This is all possible because Young Living is more of a giant family than a company since it is full of supportive, encouraging, inspirational people with the incredible D. Gary and Mary Young at the helm to guide the way. It is impossible to be a part of this movement without feeling completely connected, respected, supported, and empowered!

6. SPREAD HOPE

If you've been following my blog, you know that hope is kind of my thing, so this is definitely one of my favorite benefits of Team Young Living. With Young Living, teens can help others in infinite ways. They can help others by sharing their experience with everything else on this list, but they can also get involved with major initiatives locally, nationally, and globally thanks to the Young Living Foundation. The Young Living Foundation is one of the most incredible non-profit organizations on the planet not only because of the causes it supports, but also because 100% of all donations go directly to the causes! That is incredibly rare in the non-profit world, but not at all surprising to those of us in the Young Living family.

7. HELP SAVE THE PLANET

So many young people are passionate about saving and sustaining the environment and Young Living provides education, tools, and opportunities to really make a difference. Young Living takes sustainable farming and their stewardship of the land very seriously and their practices yield the products that ultimately replace the harmful synthetics that are doing so much damage. You can find out all about it at www.seedtoseal.com!

8. LIVE OOLA

Oola is a term coined by the amazing Dr. Troy Amdahl and Dr. Dave Braun in their book, *Oola: Find Balance in an Unbalanced World*. Oola is a state of awesomeness where your life is balanced and flowing, and Young Living has helped to turn Oola into a multi-sensory experience. Basically, Young Living teamed up with some of the coolest personal development dudes on the planet and created essential oil blends to help everyone achieve Oola. Teens can check out the book and oil up with some Balance™, Grow™, or any of the oils for the seven key areas of life – Family, Friends, Faith, Fitness, Field, Finance, and Fun. Oola is for all ages, but giving these tools to someone at the beginning of their journey into life is a surefire way to equip them for greatness!

9. Build a Business

I don't know of any other part time jobs for teens that offer limitless, willable, residual income and an opportunity to make a positive impact on countless lives, so the business opportunity is a pretty powerful reason to have Young Living in your life at any age! Teens as young as 16 can actually begin exploring the business side of Young Living by sharing their love for natural wellness with others while building a team and earning stellar compensation. It requires work and dedication for sure, but with tools like *Gameplan* by Sarah Harnish and *25 to Life* by Adam Green, it is absolutely possible for young entrepreneurs to change lives and earn money. For details, check out the 2015 Income Disclosure in Appendix A.

10. Be the Change

Many young people like to be trendsetters and there is no better trend right now than wellness, purpose, and abundance! There is a massive shift happening, but it is going to take an entire generation of people to stand up for the environment, clean living, nutrition, ethics, connection, and values. With Young Living in their life, teens can be a part of all of that, stay above the wellness line, and work to make shift happen in a positive, proactive way that benefits the Earth and all of its inhabitants.

There are many, many other reasons and we are going to revisit all of these along with some others in this guide. If you need help getting started with Young Living, reach out to the person that shared this book with you and, if you randomly happened across it, I would be happy to help you find a sponsor.

A Little Bit About Social Media...

There are many opportunities for you to explore the concepts in this guide on social media, but you can participate just as easily in your journal or right here in the book. Always talk to your parent or guardian before joining a social network and be sure to read the guidelines, practice Internet safety, and communicate with kindness.

If you are already on social media, I want you to think about what type of things you see when you go on your favorite social media sites and, more importantly, how you feel about yourself and your world after spending time scrolling through your feed.

Many people, especially young people, are starting to notice that their time online is causing them to feel overwhelmed and anxious as their feeds are inundated with controversial and often inaccurate information along with the rants, opinions, updates, and images of people who are carefully selecting everything they share. This combination often leads to negativity, fear, self-doubt, and stressful interactions with other people.

Since the uplifting and heartwarming posts are often lost in the midst of photoshopped selfies, celebrity gossip, emotional tirades, and biased propaganda, many conversations about social media tend to focus on the pitfalls and challenges that people face online.

Teachers and other authority figures often spend a lot of time and energy warning children and teens about digital dangers and, although online safety is very important, I contend that their work would be a lot easier if they spent a little more time and energy telling kids what TO do instead of only telling them what NOT to do.

In order to help shift this imbalance, I set out on a mission to find examples of positive social media for teens so that I could help you understand that you have a choice about what you focus on digitally just as you can choose what you focus on in real life. I ended up exploring the depths of an amazing digital realm devoted to bringing inspirational and meaningful messages to people of all ages.

Over the course of my experiment, I was introduced to so many stellar sites and I even ventured out of my comfort zone and visited platforms that were totally unfamiliar to me! Ultimately, I came to realize that there are hundreds, if not thousands, of powerful, positive and compassionate voices trying to make a difference and change the world for the better through the use of social media tools. I was really inspired and decided that I want to do whatever I can to help them be heard.

To help me with this mission, you can check out and follow the top ten profiles I found (Appendix B) and you can start to create your own positive content right now. At the very least, I urge you to check out something uplifting, ponder the posts, and share them with anyone who may be struggling with digital challenges.

A Little Bit about You...

Here is where we get to the heart of this guide. You're going to spend a lot of time thinking about who you are, what you believe, what choices you make, and how you fit into and impact the world around you. In honor of that journey, I want you to start with this blank page and just write down some thoughts about who you are at this moment. Be honest, but try not to be too harsh or judgmental. Embrace your quirkiness and realize that the things that make you different from others will ultimately be your biggest assets in this guide and in your life. This is for you - you're not handing this in for a grade, no one else will ever see it (unless you want them to), and your answers are subject to change as you go through the rest of the guide and as you continue on through life. Think of this as a snapshot of who you are today. Write anything and everything that pops into your head and remember the questions are only there as a guide if you get stuck or need a place to start. Here are some prompts to help you get started.

What is your life like?

What do you get really excited about?

What makes you angry or frustrated?

What stories have shaped you up until this point?

ALL ABOUT ME:

YOU MATTER

HELLO. MY NAME IS _____ AND I MATTER.

If you only take one thing away from this guide, I hope it is the message from this section. Regardless of what you wrote on the previous page, where you choose to go from here, what decisions you've made, or the condition of your life circumstances – you matter!

Understanding and embracing wellness will not make you matter any more than you already do, but it can definitely help you realize, understand, and ultimately love and accept yourself so you can live from that place of empowerment.

This is the most important concept in the guide, but it is also the most difficult. If someone had told me to love myself when I was a teen, I would've laughed at them, told them that it was selfish and conceited to think that way, and changed the topic immediately before anyone noticed that I barely even liked myself, and that the concept of self-love was as mythical as a unicorn.

As we continue to work through the rest of the activities in this guide, I'm going to refer back to your self-assessment on page 27 and I'm going to keep reminding you of these big goals of self-acceptance and self-love because this is a process and a journey. Allow it to be messy, be gentle with yourself, look for the good stuff, and stick with me because I have a feeling you will end up surprising yourself before we are done.

WHAT MATTERS

Now that we've discussed how valuable you are and how much you matter, I'm going to take a little break from being your biggest cheerleader and get you to start digging into the things that matter most to you. This section is going to set the foundation for the rest of the guide because you are going to need a find a few good reasons to stay focused when things get boring or overwhelming.

Make a list of ten things that matter the most to you. You can choose from absolutely anything, but they should all be things that you wouldn't want to live without - friends, family, sports, hobbies, music, games, books, etc.

1.

2.

3.

4.

5.

6.

7.

8.

9.

10.

Now put a star next to everything on that list that you could enjoy even more if you felt good all the time and had awesome health and wellness. All of those stars can lead you to your "why".

WHAT IS YOUR "WHY"?

Simon Sinek has a great TEDTalk about the power of "why" and I highly recommend it. You can find it on YouTube as "Start with Why - Simon Sinek TEDTalk". Basically, Simon Sinek and many other great motivators and leaders have come to the conclusion that it is important to have a really good reason for doing something before you begin, because you can remember that reason when things get tough. So, in addition to your list of ten above, I also want you to think about WHY you want more wellness, purpose, and/or abundance in your life.

This might be difficult if you're reading this book because someone asked you to, but it's never too late to create a meaningful connection, so spend some time with this one.

Finish this sentence -

I want to feel good, be more confident in my choices, discover my passion and purpose, and/or help others and myself in a really big way because

_____

_____

_____

_____

_____

_____

It doesn't matter if your "why" focuses on sports, success in school, an important person in your life or anything else - it only matters that you are choosing to explore some new territory to get a better idea of who you are and how you can take better care of yourself. The details of your "why" may evolve and change as you get further into the guide and they will almost definitely shift as you get older and that is okay.

OBSTACLES AND OPPORTUNITIES

Now that you have an idea of the things that matter to you and you're starting to think a little more about what motivates you to do the things you do, I want you to take a step back and start thinking about where you want to go because that vision is going to help you navigate the obstacles and embrace the opportunities. No matter where your life takes you, there will always be obstacles, or things that get in your way and slow you down, and there will always be opportunities to learn, grow, and help others.

Unfortunately, the obstacles that young people encounter today can have serious and often life-altering consequences, so I want you to know that I'm not discounting or ignoring the reality of peer pressure, bullying, school stress, abuse, addiction, self-harm, suicide, sexual pressures, or anything else that you might be facing. I am, however, hoping to get you to see that there are many alternative realities that can improve your life and maybe even the world around you.

The rest of this guide is about wellness, purpose, and abundance and it is entirely possible that you haven't really spent any time thinking about those three things, so they might all feel like obstacles. To be honest, the majority of teens I work with aren't thinking about the state of their minds, bodies, and spirits in the context of wellness, so you're already ahead of the game.

Many young people struggle with judgments about their minds being too scattered, their bodies being the wrong size or shape, and their connections to themselves and others being too superficial. Those judgments are just a few examples of the obstacles that can be turned into opportunities, but this is not easy, so be patient with yourself and everyone else involved.

As Tony Robbins says, "If you want to look for obstacles, what's wrong is always available. But, so is what's right!" This is one of my favorite quotes because it reminds me to look for the opportunities and it helps me to look at the challenges differently too. This principle works in all different ways and I'm sure you can even hop on Tumblr right now and find a kazillion quotes about the challenges in life, but you can also find just as many about the promise of joy and miracles.

The main difference in what you find comes from what you go looking for and what you focus on, but it also comes from knowing that you have the power to turn any obstacle into an opportunity to learn and grow.

Challenges and obstacles are not put in our path to stop us, they are put there to stretch our limits and to show us what we are really capable of, which is definitely something to celebrate.

As you flip through the rest of this guide, you will be challenged, and there may be obstacles, but I know you will be able to see all of the opportunities if you allow yourself to look for the possibilities

You can even apply this theory in your everyday life outside of this guide. The next time you find yourself wondering "why is this happening to me?" try switching it to "what can I learn from this?" and see how much better it feels! Then, jot down your experiences as a reminder for the next time you feel stuck.

MY OBSTACLE:

HOW I TURNED IT INTO AN OPPORTUNITY:

CHOICES

I've moved this part around a few times because it connects with all of the other sections. I decided to move it toward the front because without a basic understanding of the power of choice, the rest of this guide is pretty useless.

I was in high school the first time someone pointed out to me that we don't always get to choose what happens to us, but we always get to choose how we react. At first, I tried to argue and point out how I couldn't help getting angry, sad, mad or frustrated when bad things happened. Thankfully, I ultimately realized that no one else could choose my thoughts for me and no situation was more powerful than my ability to choose positive, or at least constructive, thoughts.

We all make dozens of choices every day, from what we wear and eat to the people we interact with, the hobbies we have, the sports we play and so much more. We also make choices about what we focus on, what we put in and on our bodies, how we connect with others, how we perceive ourselves and others, and about a million other things. Even deciding not to choose is still a choice, so our days are literally filled with choices, both conscious and subconscious. The rest of this guide is going to help you focus on making the best choices for you, so you can be happy, serve others, and maybe even experience some miracles.

One of my favorite definitions for miracle is choosing love instead of fear. After I heard that definition, I realized that there are so many opportunities to choose love - especially in situations that are annoying, scary, boring, or stressful. I am inspired to choose love thanks to a really brave mom, Scarlett Lewis, who has used the death of her young son, Jesse, to teach people all over the world about forgiveness and about choosing love.

Check out her book *Nurturing, Healing, Love* if you want to know more about her incredible journey and be sure to find the Jesse Lewis Choose Love Movement on social media, too!

Your first choice happens right now as you choose to go on to the next page and be a pioneer in the world of mind, body, and spirit wellness for teens. I hope you choose to stick around!

WELLNESS

Now that you've explored your why, thought about some broad obstacles and opportunities and learned that you have the power to choose how you react, we will explore some of the ways you can use wellness to create your best life.

At this point you might be intrigued, but you might also be wondering why this idea of wellness is up to YOU. It is awesome to have parents, loved ones, and teachers to help guide and care for us, but when it comes to real wellness, the choices you make as a teen are incredibly important. If you can operate a tablet, smartphone, laptop, video game or anything else that requires batteries, you should also know how to take care of the most miraculous devices on the planet – your mind, body, and spirit.

The key to this whole wellness thing is moderation and balance, so you're going to see those two words a lot as we explore different topics. There really can be too much of a good thing if we are talking about things like food, exercise, and sleep, and it's easy to go to extremes and get out of balance if we aren't connected in body, mind and spirit. The goal of this section is for you to acknowledge different types of toxins while realizing how much power you have to choose non-toxic alternatives for everything from food to friends.

WELLNESS VS. ILLNESS

Wellness may be a relatively new concept for you, and that's okay. Much of our society likes to focus on illness, so having an adventure into the wonders of wellness may seem a little weird at first. Ironically, many people spend time taking their cars in for oil changes and making sure they're always road ready, but they don't really think about how they're feeling until they are not feeling well. If we treated our cars the way we treat our bodies, we wouldn't think about what they needed until the check engine light came on. For the most part, we don't call the doctor when we're feeling well; we call when we're already sick.

Learning about proactive wellness was definitely one of the hardest parts of my journey so far because, like a lot of people, I was very *reactive* to my health and focused on it only when there was an illness. When something hurt or didn't feel good, I tried to fix it. Although a large number of people operate from that perspective, I'm incredibly grateful to have found ways to be *proactive*. By learning to take care of my body and all of its systems before something goes wrong, it not only feels great to keep my focus in this positive place, it actually keeps me well!

Remember that I am not a medical doctor or a mental health professional, so we are going to be focusing on some basic tips and tricks to keep you feeling amazing. If you are experiencing any serious or intense physical, mental, or emotional challenges, please be sure to schedule an appointment with the appropriate healthcare provider.

SELF-CARE 101

"I can take care of myself!" is something I hear all the time from my 5 year old and, as much as I'm surprised by his independence some days, I really do want him to know that it is important for us to take care of ourselves. Many times, we get caught up in helping and caring for other people and we forget to do the things that will keep us feeling our best. Although this is normal and natural, it is another thing we need to keep in balance because it is impossible to pour from an empty cup -- we need to make sure we fill ourselves up so that we have plenty to give to others.

I love the analogy of the oxygen mask on the airplane. For those of you who have flown before, you know that they tell you to secure your own oxygen mask before helping anyone else, and that's because we can't help others if we aren't breathing ourselves. As we move through the upcoming sections – especially the ones about purpose – we need to remember this analogy so we don't burn out or get too overwhelmed.

That personal oxygen mask might look a little different to each person, but there are some basic tips that can keep us feeling good and filling our cups. For the purpose of this brief guide, we are going to focus on healthy habits for our body, mind and spirit along with awareness of the toxins that we encounter every day.

SOME SELF-CARE TIPS TO START YOUR JOURNEY

- Take some time for yourself every day – schedule it if you need to
- Remember that self-care is not selfish
- Be aware of your environment and everything in it (this includes people)
- Be gentle with yourself – especially if you are in a tough situation where you don't have many options
- Small habits over time make the biggest differences
- _____
- _____

FEELING GOOD NATURALLY

We already discussed the idea that we don't always get to choose what happens to us, but since we do get to choose how we react and we can also choose our actions, we can look for things that make us feel good.

Feeling good naturally is one of the key ideas in this guide and it is also where things are going to get a little more fun in terms of social media connections. Since feeling good is a little different for everyone, there will be plenty of opportunities to draw your own conclusions, connect to your favorite things, and even create some great posts or new hashtags!

Unfortunately, the quest to feel good leads a lot of teens down the wrong path because they seek danger, drugs, sex, self-harm, gambling, or other destructive behaviors. Adrenaline and drug-induced highs can numb challenging situations and give false impressions of good feelings. We are going to explore some ways to ditch those destructive decisions and choose safe and natural alternatives.

The main thing we have to remember is that the goal is to ditch the toxins – toxic products, toxic people, and toxic choices – the rest is completely customizable.

In order to come up with the custom plan that works best for you, we are going to talk about how to support our minds, bodies, and spirits with a few simple tips, tricks, and, of course, essential oils!

Patty's Top Tricks for Feeling Good without Toxins, Drugs, or Alcohol

- Breathe
- Choose Healthy Foods
- Sleep Well
- Gratitude/Prayer/Meditation
- Play with Play-Doh
- Go Outside
- Create Something
- Listen to Music
- Unplug and Connect in Real Life
- Oil Up *Huh? What is that?! Stay tuned… that is coming.*
- _____
- _____

WHAT THINGS ON THIS LIST SOUND GOOD TO YOU?

WHAT DO YOU DO TO FEEL GOOD?

Make your own list of ways to feel good without toxins, drugs or alcohol. If you have trouble coming up with ten, that's okay - you're in the right place! List what you can -- the important part is to start the conversation.

Of those things you listed, put a star by the ones that are a little more difficult to do when you're tired, stressed or anxious.

1.

2.

3.

4.

5.

6.

7.

8.

9.

10.

"There's an Oil for That!" Intro to Essential Oils

This is where we step outside of the usual "eat right, get sleep, breathe, and go outside" advice and step into a topic that may be completely new territory for some of you. As you all know, new territory might seem a little funny or "weird" so this is one of those places where I want you to keep an open mind and explore your options a little -- remember, the fun stuff usually happens outside your comfort zone!!

What is an Essential Oil?

Essential oils are powerful liquids that are carefully extracted from plants, trees, shrubs, roots, fruits, and herbs through a process called distillation. Essential oils have been used throughout recorded history to support all of the systems of the human body as well as the mind and the spirit. They are referred to as the lifeblood of a plant because they are the most powerful part of the plant and perform many of the same functions in a plant as our blood performs in our bodies.

There are three ways you can use essential oils and as you explore and experiment, you will find what works best for you. There is no right or wrong way to use the oils that are recommended to support your journey to wellness, so enjoy the exploration and remember that all of my suggestions apply only to Young Living essential oils.

1. Topical - apply 2-3 drops directly to your skin either alone (neat) or mixed with a pure vegetable "carrier" oil. My favorite carrier oils are Young Living's V-6™ and organic coconut oil.
2. Aromatic - rub a few drops in your hands and inhale, use 5-7 drops in a diffuser, or place a few drops on a cotton ball and put it in a vent in your house or car.
3. Internal - Each Young Living oil is labeled as to how it may be used, and you can use the entire Vitality™ line of oils in your favorite drink, in a vegetable capsule, or as an ingredient when you are cooking.

Are Essential Oils Safe and Effective?

This is a tricky question because not all oils are created equal. Interestingly, there is an overall answer that addresses both parts of this question. If you know where your oils are sourced from and that they are 100% pure, they are both safe and effective.

Many people have tried essential oils from the drug store or the grocery store with little or no effect and in some cases the oils have even caused discomfort! Since there is no regulation in the oil industry in our country, an oil bottle only needs to contain 5% essential oil in order to be labeled "100% pure"! That means that up to 95% could be synthetic, which defeats the entire purpose of choosing a toxin-free lifestyle.

After doing extensive research on all of the oil companies on the market, I chose Young Living Essential Oils because they were the only ones that guarantee the purity and potency with complete transparency. They guarantee their entire process from Seed to Seal™ and you can find out all about it at www.seedtoseal.com.

Young Living has hundreds of oils to choose from and they are available as singles, which means the oil is only from one plant, or blends, which are a combination of oils from two or more different plants. Even though there are hundreds of oils, they are very versatile so you only need about 10-20 to have a good collection. I recommend getting started with one of Young Living's Premium Starter Kits so that you can save money and have a great selection. I'm sure whomever shared this book with you would be happy to help you get a kit, so be sure to connect with them before you order.

As far as safety is concerned, the same information is important. Pure oils are incredibly safe – especially when compared to their toxic counterparts. However, there are a few safety precautions that I want to include before you begin your oily journey.

- Start low and go slow. Oils are incredibly potent -- a little bit goes a long way and you can use an organic carrier oil like Young Living's V-6™ or organic coconut oil to dilute and spread the oils further. Always dilute with a carrier oil for small children and most pets.

- Avoid contact with sensitive areas.
- Some oils are photosensitive, so read the labels. This usually pertains to citrus oils like lemon, grapefruit, and bergamot, but those oils are included in many blends, so be careful with sun exposure if you're applying any of those oils directly to your skin.
- As always, if you have a disease or medical condition or if you are taking prescription drugs, it is recommended that you consult with a healthcare professional who has experience with essential oils.

WHY WOULD I WANT TO TRY ESSENTIAL OILS?

There are so many reasons, but here are a few that might mean the most to you:

- They are a safe, natural, toxin-free alternative to the synthetic, chemical-laden products made by companies that target us as consumers.
- They help us to rest well and relax so stress doesn't have such a profound impact.
- They smell awesome and make us feel good.
- We need to exercise our right to choose something safe for our families and ourselves and so we can ditch the toxins that are creating untold challenges for us physically, mentally, and emotionally.

This is a very brief intro and overview of oils because there are countless resources that you can get for free online to further develop your understanding of oils and their amazing properties. My favorite online overview is definitely the Essential Oils 101 audio by Sarah Harnish at www.oilabilityteam.com.

Now that you know WHAT essential oils are, we are going to explore how they can support your journey to wellness in three key areas - body, mind, and spirit. In addition to my favorite oil suggestions, I'm also going to share other tips that will get you closer to the overall goals of feeling good and living toxin-free.

The most important thing I want you to know while you explore wellness in terms of essential oils and also in context with your unique body, mind, and spirit is this:

YOU HAVE OPTIONS

As I mentioned, you will continue to see my favorite essential oil suggestions for supporting overall wellness as you work with each topic. It doesn't matter if you choose to use them topically or aromatically (as long as you follow the safety guidelines). You do not need the essential oils in order to do the activities, they are not intended to treat or cure any conditions, there are no right or wrong oils for supporting personal growth, and I tried to include at least one starter kit product in each section. If you do choose to use the oils, I have included blank lines for you to add your favorite choices. Last but not least, check out the References and Resources section at the very back of this book to find more books, websites, YouTube channels and apps that will help you to learn even more about the products.

#TeenOiler Testimonial
Taylor Age 13

"When I first heard about essential oils I thought that they didn't work and it was dumb. Back then I used to feel sad and down. I would also have a hard time keeping track of my schoolwork. When I finally tried them I found that they actually worked. I really can feel the positive changes Young Living made in my life. I use them when I'm doing art, I use them during school, and I use them when I'm sad. The bonus of using the oils is that they are natural and good for your body. So I'm now living a better and healthier lifestyle."

Wellness for Your Body

We are going to explore physical wellness first because it is a lot easier to take care of our mind and spirit when our bodies are working efficiently and feeling good. Unfortunately, it is getting a lot more challenging to get our bodies the fuel they need from food because of toxins and a lack of nutrients in the soil. While it is practically impossible to avoid all toxins, we can find ways to be more aware of them and to incorporate supplements and other products that will help balance everything. In this section, we will learn a little more about toxins and then explore good choices for nutrition, exercise, personal care, and overall body image.

Let's Talk Toxins

My goal isn't to freak you out, but I'm going to have to add an exception in this case, because I don't think we can talk about toxins without freaking out just a little.

We live in a very toxic society and according to the Natural Resources Defense Council, "Of the more than 80,000 chemicals currently used in the United States, most haven't been adequately tested for their effects on human health. These chemicals lurk in everyday items: furniture, cosmetics, household cleaners, toys, even food."!!

According to the Center for Disease Control (CDC), cancer is the number two cause of death in the United States and the majority of those deaths are from factors that are under our control with only 5-10% of cases being from genetic defects. That means that many cancer cases in the U.S. are directly linked to poor diet, physical inactivity, weight or chemical exposure.

We are going to explore nutrition, exercise, and some known toxins, but I highly recommend checking out the Environmental Working Group's (EWG's) list of the "Dirty Dozen" toxins that are found in our everyday lives. Some of these will sound familiar to you and others will sound like they are in another language, but you should be aware of them as you begin to look at labels and think more about the things you use every day.

1. BPA
2. Dioxin
3. Atrazine
4. Phthalates
5. Perchlorate
6. Fire Retardants
7. Lead
8. Arsenic
9. Mercury
10. Perfluorinated chemicals (PFCs)
11. Organophosphate pesticides
12. Glycol Ethers

I know that some of these toxins sound really weird, but you don't need to be a scientist to understand them because the EWG website breaks it all down and explains where they can be found and how to avoid them. You can visit their website at www.ewg.org to find out more about this list as well as other toxins in everything from food and water to cleaning products, children's toys, and personal care products.

PERSONAL CARE PRODUCTS

This is a tough one. If you're like me and millions of other people on the planet, you probably love your hair products, beauty products, and makeup. I was a self-proclaimed product junkie for most of my life and this has been the most challenging (and slowest) transformation for me. Thanks to a cool app called *THINK DIRTY*, I am able to know what is in my products before I buy them and I have definitely replaced a lot of my favorite things with toxin-free varieties from Young Living. Like I said, I didn't do this all at once. I started with one item at a time as I ran out of my regular products and some things, like makeup, have taken longer because Young Living doesn't have a full makeup line. Luckily, one of the amazing Crown Diamond leaders, Melissa Poepping, also created a toxin-free makeup line called "Sweet Savvy Minerals" that you can check out at www.sweetsavvyminerals.com!

PATTY'S FAVORITE PERSONAL CARE PRODUCTS FROM YOUNG LIVING

- Thieves Aromabright™ Toothpaste
- Aromaguard Meadow Mist Deodorant™
- Evening Peace™ Bath and Shower Gel
- Grapefruit Lip Balm
- Lavender Hand & Body Lotion
- Orange Blossom Facial Wash
- Satin Facial Scrub
- Copaiba Vanilla Moisturizing Shampoo & Conditioner
- Valor™ Moisturizing Soap

NUTRITION

So far, we've mentioned a lot of harmful toxins in the environment and explored how important it is to pay attention to what we put ON our body, and now we are going to explore the importance of what we put IN our body.

As I mentioned in the beginning of this section, moderation is definitely the key to wellness in all areas. You're going to see that over and over in this guide because in some cases, there really can be too much of a good thing.

Book stores, libraries, magazines, newspapers and the Internet are filled with diet suggestions, food recommendations, recipes, advice and photographs. It's very important that you apply the same theory to all of that input as you do to the advice within this guide. Take what works for you, and leave the rest. To revisit the car analogy, though, food is fuel. If you want your body to be in peak condition and running on all cylinders, you need to be sure you fill it with appropriate amounts of nutritious food.

PATTY'S NUTRITION TIPS

- Perfection is not the goal
- Stick with things that you can pronounce
- Take good quality vitamins and supplements
- Eat less processed food
- Eat more vegetables - especially green ones
- Choose organic foods whenever possible
- Cut down on (or eliminate) sugar
- Keep track of what you're eating (digitally or on paper)
- Listen to your body
- Plan ahead so you can have healthy options
- _____
- _____
- _____

ESSENTIAL OILS TO SUPPORT NUTRITION AND DIGESTION

- Lemon
- Grapefruit
- Peppermint
- DiGize™
- Any of the Vitality™ oils
- _____
- _____

OTHER NUTRITIONAL PRODUCTS FROM YOUNG LIVING:

THE NINGXIA LINE

According to the Young Living Product Guide, "For more than 700 years, the northwest region of China known as Ningxia has earned a reputation for producing and cultivating premium wolfberries. Also known as gogi berries, wolfberries have a rich nutritional profile. Ningxia Red™ is our powerful superfruit supplement designed to energize, fortify, and revitalize the body and mind."

My family likes to start our day with a shot of Ningxia Red™ and Ningxia Nitro™ was even acknowledged in the beginning of this guide! Ningxia Zyng* is a carbonated drink and you can even eat the dried wolfberries, too! If you currently drink soda or other energy drinks, you'll definitely want to try these nutritious and natural alternatives!

EINKORN

Einkorn grain is an ancient grain that hasn't been modified or hybridized so it has tons of great nutrients and is more gentle on the digestive system than many other modern grains. You can experience it in flour, pancake and waffle mix and spaghetti and you can learn more about it in D. Gary Young's Book *Ancient Einkorn: Today's Staff of Life.*

NUTRITIONAL SUPPLEMENTS

"Vitamins and minerals are two of the foundations of a healthy diet. However, diet alone often cannot provide sufficient amounts of these important nutrients. Our convenient multivitamin supplement solutions feature bioavailable food-sourced vitamins and minerals that contain an infusion of powerful essential oils to give you the support you need." Young Living 2016 Product Guide

Everyone's individual needs are different, but certain supplements like probiotics and Vitamin C can definitely support wellness for most of us. If you have questions about supplements, please check with your doctor and visit the YouTube page (@thefarmacistala) for Dr. Lindsey Elmore because she explains things really well!

SOCIAL MEDIA CHALLENGE

Everyone loves food pictures! Snap a shot of some fresh veggies or other healthy food and inspire others to find some nutrition, too! Bonus points if it's a meal you prepare yourself!

#TEENOILER TESTIMONIAL
SIERA AGE 18
"I started using oils about two years ago and they have helped me immensely. Oils have been able to help me with things as small as stress from school, all the way to supporting my immune system through some times in my life. There is no doubt oils have been a huge part of helping me through the last two years of my life."

NUTRITION EXPLORATION

Write down everything you eat for three days in one column and write how you feel in the other column. The goal with this activity is to get you to notice the effect different foods have on your mood and energy levels.

	FOOD	FEELING
DAY 1		
DAY 2		
DAY 3		

EXERCISE

This isn't one of my strongest areas, but I know it is important. So, you're going to see that my tips are a little more vague and there are fewer of them, but I'm leaving it here for a few reasons. It is important for you to see that we all still have some things to learn and I also want you to see that I'm trying to grow in this area and that I'm owning the fact that there are lots of other people who would be able to help. This is one of the seeds that I'm planting, but it is definitely up to you to water it.

If you like sports and are on a team, you may be ahead of the game on this, but organized sports aren't your only option when it comes to exercise. There are choices that range from recreational league teams to cable channels that provide exercise advice in short increments that you can watch from the comfort of your couch. Well, you may want to get off the couch, but even if you're not active, you can always choose to be more active. Let's work on this together.

PATTY'S EXERCISE TIPS

- Make a goal to move your body for at least 30 minutes a day.
- Stretch
- Stay hydrated
- Make it social
- Find a good mentor/trainer/coach/role model
- Do something that you enjoy
- Keep track of your accomplishments (digitally or on paper)
- _____
- _____

ESSENTIAL OILS TO SUPPORT FITNESS

- Oola Fitness™
- Peppermint
- Copaiba
- Deep Relief™
- Cool Azul™
- _____
- _____

YOUNG LIVING PRODUCTS FOR ATHLETES

Many of Young Living's brand ambassadors are incredible athletes like James Lawrence, the "Iron Cowboy", former NFL player, Stevie Baggs Jr, and Iditarod Champion, Mitch Seavey. Since these athletes perform extreme feats, they need the best nutrition, supplements, and essential oils. Here are a few products they recommend:

- Chocolate Deluxe Pure Protein Complete™
- NingXia Zyng™
- Tea Tree (Melaleuca Alternifolia)
- Thieves™
- Lemon Vitality™
- PanAway™
- RC™
- Idaho Balsam Fir
- Copaiba

SOCIAL MEDIA CHALLENGE

Find and follow an inspirational coach, trainer or athlete so you can receive their reminders and get excited about exercise! I love the Iron Cowboy, James Lawrence and Jillian Michaels. Start a group with friends on Facebook, irunurun, or MyFitnessPal! Share your workouts, post the steps your FitBit records, and inspire each other to reach your goals! Bonus: Who motivates you?

MOVEMENT TRACKER

In case social media isn't your thing, you can definitely track your goals right here in your guide. Make sure you notice how your body feels and how your mood and energy are impacted by exercise!

	WHAT YOU DID	HOW YOU FELT
DAY 1		
DAY 2		
DAY 3		
DAY 4		
DAY 5		
DAY 6		
DAY 7		

HEALTHY BODY IMAGE

Although I've tried to separate mind, body, and spirit for this section, the truth is that each realm is intricately connected to the others. I wasn't sure if body image would go in the body or mind section, but it feels at home right here between the two.

This is another area that I struggle with and I feel that it is really important for me to be honest with you in these sections because I don't want to give you the false impression that I have it all figured out. There is always room for us to grow, no matter where we are on our path.

I'm wayyyyyyy further along now than I was as a chubby middle-schooler with big red glasses, but I also love the power of Instagram and Snapchat filters to hide blemishes, bad hair days and those fluffy parts of my body. Just like food and exercise, I think filters also need to be added to the moderation list because it is easy to lose touch with ourselves and with reality when we are constantly enhancing everything with apps and digital tools.

The media even takes this to an extreme as you can see in the viral YouTube video, "Body Evolution - Model Before and After". Photoshop has become the standard for changing the appearance of celebrities, people in advertisements -- even family portraits. This phenomenon creates some really unrealistic body image standards for both girls and boys. Thankfully, many people are starting to take a stand and celebrate body diversity. My favorite site is www.bodyimagemovement.com where you can find out a lot about body acceptance and learn more about the "Embrace" documentary.

One of my favorite quotes, from Marcia Hutchinson, is "If you talked to your friends the way you talk to your body, you would have no friends left at all." Next time you're watching your favorite TV show or movie, take notice of the people in the background. They're all different shapes and sizes; there is no one body shape with perfect proportions, but you can definitely pick out the healthy people and the unhealthy people by the way they move. Not all of the unhealthy people are overweight, and not all of the healthy people are thin. Your challenges when it comes to your body image might be hereditary, or they might be the result of your environment or choices you've made, but you always have the choice to forgive yourself for any mistakes, and treat yourself with the same respect you would treat a friend. Louise Hay has done some great work on body image and loving yourself, using mirror exercises. Look at yourself in the mirror and say "I Love You" to your reflection until you begin to believe it. If you crack up the first few times, that's okay. You're in the right place. Do it again tomorrow and every day.

Essential Oils To support a healthy body image

- Oola Friends™
- Oola Family™
- Gathering™
- Frankincense
- Acceptance™
- Release™
- Valor™/Valor II™
- _____

Social Media Challenge

Watch and share the music video for "Try" by Colbie Caillat and then take your own all-natural selfie with no makeup and no filters to celebrate yourself exactly how you are #nofilter #naturalselfie

#DitchandSwitch Challenge

Now that you've had some time to explore full body wellness in a few different contexts, I want to come back to the idea of toxins and challenge you to make some conscious choices to eliminate those toxic elements from your personal care products, food, activities and even your thoughts because that will get you ready for the next section!

	Toxic Choice	Natural Choice
Personal Care Product		
Food		
Activity		
Thought		

WELLNESS FOR YOUR MIND

Keeping our minds in good shape is just as important as keeping our bodies in shape, but the strategies aren't quite as obvious as eating well and exercising (although those things will also do a lot to support a healthy mind). Being proactive in terms of our minds is a really in-depth topic, so we are going to touch on some of the basics and then you're going to have some room to explore.

Our minds are incredibly powerful and I have come to learn that Napoleon Hill was absolutely correct when he said, "Whatever the mind can conceive and believe, it can achieve." The tricky part is that this concept works in both positive and negative directions, so we need to make sure that we are practicing ways to keep our minds conceiving and believing in things that we want and not in the things that we don't want.

At first, it might be hard to accept the fact that we can choose our thoughts, especially if you've never really slowed down long enough to think about your thinking. This is also a tough concept if your experience with thinking and learning has been limited to what you do in school – especially if those experiences haven't been particularly positive.

Basically, if we want to feel good, we need to choose thoughts that make us feel good, but that is a lot easier said than done - especially once momentum takes over. I'm sure you've experienced the momentum of thought when you wake up late, struggle to find your clothes, miss breakfast, and the rest of your day continues to ride the energy of that negative train. That is how "bad days" happen and it is also how epic days happen when we focus on our blessings and see all of the good things that are happening.

Now that you've realized how the momentum of your thoughts helps to determine the kind of day you're going to have, you can begin to implement some of the techniques in this section to slow your thoughts down and choose better ones that will create the kind of day (and life) that you want. Thankfully, this is a process and no one expects you to master it immediately, but you can start playing around with it right now and see how it feels.

This section is packed full of introductions to great concepts and tips and I hope you will choose to explore each one a little more deeply as you begin to practice the basics outlined here. First, we are going to talk about some general cognitive support to help you focus and remember things better in and out of school. Then we are going to explore good and bad stress as well as the effects of bad stress. Next we are going to explore beliefs, mindfulness, and goal setting. Finally, we will wrap everything up with two of my favorite tools, Oola and the AromaFreedom Technique.

Brain Stuff

I started to call this section "cognitive functions" but didn't want that showing up in the Table of Contents and freaking anyone out... Basically, cognitive functions are things that we do with our brains – things like language, reasoning, memory, and attention. All of these things help us to learn and think, so keeping our brains healthy is pretty important.

Earlier I mentioned your experiences with thinking and learning as part of your education, so I wanted to make sure that I offered a few tips for learning along with my favorite Young Living products to support focus and clarity.

Patty's memory and learning tips:

- Try different strategies until you find what works best for you
- Discover your learning style
- Pace yourself
- Avoid comparison and judgment
- Remember that learning can and should be FUN!
- _____

Essential Oils to Support Cognitive Function

- Brain Power™
- Clarity™
- GeneYus™
- Frankincense
- _____

51

Stress

"I'm sooooooo stressed out!" This is probably the most common reply I've ever gotten when I ask teens how they are doing. As true as it probably is, I can't help but wonder why so many of you get stressed and stay stuck there. So far, my theory is that you don't have the tools or techniques to get unstuck and that your diet and sleep habits are probably compounding the situation so your mind and body never get a break. So, our goal throughout this section is to get you to slow down a little and get to a place where your body can rest and recover well enough to give your mind a much-needed break. Sounds pretty good, right?

Good Stress vs. Bad Stress

Before we get to a place where our bodies and minds can take a break, it helps to understand that not all stress is created equal and not all stress is bad. In our culture, we have given stress a very negative connotation by connecting it with overwhelm and burnout, but there are good kinds of stress that actually motivate us and help us to improve.

If it weren't for the good kind of stress, I never would've been able to finish this book and some people wouldn't even be able to get out of bed in the morning. However, the good stress is short term and mild whereas the bad stress, or distress, is more long term and can have a serious negative impact on the body.

Our stress response, also referred to as our "fight or flight" response, is a really good thing that helps us get out of the way of danger, but it can become detrimental to our overall wellness if our bodies stay in that mode for too long - especially when there is no real danger.

#TeenOiler Testimonial
Tim Age 19

"For a while I dealt with the fact that I couldn't sleep through the night and if I did it wasn't a sound sleep. I bounced around from option to option but then I was introduced to Copaiba, which has greatly helped, in my sleep patterns. Not only did this help with my sleeping, but it did help with stress and being able to relax if I was feeling jumpy or nervous about something."

PATTY'S STRESS MANAGEMENT TIPS:

- Practice Mindfulness
- Color, draw - be creative!
- Say "no" when you need to
- Laugh, play - have fun!
- Ask for help
- Learn from mistakes
- Challenge yourself
- Set goals
- Never stop learning
- Always do your best
- Unplug
- _____

ESSENTIAL OILS TO SUPPORT RELAXATION

- Lavender
- Stress Away™
- Tranquil™
- Grounding™
- Valor™/Valor 2™
- Peace and Calming™/Peace and Calming 2™
- _____
- _____

SOCIAL MEDIA CHALLENGE

Choose your favorite feed (Instagram, Twitter, Snapchat, Musical.ly) and notice how you feel about the first five posts you see. Do they make you feel any stress? If so, is it good stress or bad stress?

Fixed Mindset vs. Growth Mindset

Before we can explore wellness for our minds too deeply, it is important to first explore our mindset. Some people have a fixed mindset, which means that they believe that our abilities and our ability to achieve and succeed are fixed because our basic qualities like intelligence and talent are fixed. These people believe that whatever we are born with is what we get and there is no way to achieve or experience any more than that.

Others have a growth mindset. People with a growth mindset are more optimistic and focused on improving and developing themselves. These people believe that intelligence and talent can be developed with hard work and dedication and they see failure as part of the learning process. These people are also the ones who tend to achieve the most success and innovation.

Why do you think people with a growth mindset are generally more successful?

What kind of mindset do you have?

If you have a fixed mindset right now, please keep reading. I hope you will find something that clicks, and allows you to see that growth and development lead to resiliency and success. Overall, this book is full of tips to develop a growth mindset, but here are a few more specifically aimed at that goal.

PATTY'S TIPS FOR DEVELOPING A GROWTH MINDSET

- Try new things
- Let go of the need to be perfect
- Enjoy the process
- Realize that failure is part of the process
- Don't seek validation
- Reflect more
- Turn "I can't do that" into "I can't do that - YET"
- _____
- _____

ESSENTIAL OILS TO SUPPORT A GROWTH MINDSET

- Frankincense
- Oola Grow™
- Inspiration™
- Motivation™
- Build Your Dream™
- Into the Future™
- _____
- _____

SOCIAL MEDIA CHALLENGE

What would you try if you knew you wouldn't fail? Share your thoughts in an image or in 150 characters or less. Bonus points for a fun hashtag!

#TeenOiler Testimonial
Brandon Age 12

"I really think other teens should know Young Living oils is stress relieving and help you focus more. I think the best thing about Young Living is that is makes toxic free and chemical free oils. I just realized that oils are a really big part of my life."

POSITIVE IS POWERFUL

I am a positive person. Actually, I probably take that to an extreme. My optimism and positivity are sometimes questioned, but I assure you that they are genuine and sincere. However, I'm not entirely certain those qualities would be as obvious if I hadn't experienced so many challenges throughout my life.

Don't get me wrong, I'm not saying that you have to have challenges in order to be genuinely happy and optimistic and I'm also not saying that having challenges leads to positivity. I am just saying that my personal journey has shown me a lot of amazing things and a lot of tragic things and I know that it all really did happen for a reason.

I have seen and done more things in the past 35 years than most people ever even dream of and I have also endured some struggles that could be classified as nightmares, but, through it all, one thing has remained constant – my smile.

I get questioned about my smile on a regular basis and my answers have covered all of the bases from being lazy (it takes more muscles to frown) to having a lot to smile about and knowing that it pisses off the miserable people. Here is the real answer – I choose to smile.

We all get to make little choices like whether or not to smile on a daily basis, but those choices aren't generally emphasized because life is busy and smiling probably isn't at the top of most people's to-do lists. At this point in my life, it is not on my to-do list either, but its automatic presence gives a lot of people the wrong impression of me.

In my quest to share the power of positivity, I generally omit the negative and that is starting to become detrimental. I suppose it is logical to focus on the good if you want others to understand how amazing it feels to have positive energy, but the people who need to experience that feeling the most are not going to be able to connect because it will sound like ignoring problems or pretending to be happy unless it is placed in the proper context.

It turns out there are some pretty common assumptions that happy people are either incredibly lucky, living perfect lives, delusional, faking it, or in denial. Although I'm sure there are plenty of people who fall into those categories, there are a lot more people who are positive because they chose to focus on the good instead of the bad.

Bad things happen to all of us. Literally. I can't think of one person that I know who hasn't been subject to some sort of challenge, bad luck, tragedy, or trauma. Yet, everyone *chooses* what he or she does with those negative experiences.

On one hand, it frustrates me to think that I have to give my attitude street cred by backing it up with the painful parts of my past. On the other hand, it does help the pain to know that I can use it for a purpose. Ultimately, I know that I've healed some pretty deep wounds and I'm happy to share pieces of that process in this guide because if even one person could find hope because of my experiences, it will somehow make them all worthwhile.

I wish the abstract ideas that I gained from my personal experiences about positivity, acceptance, forgiveness, self-love, and service were enough on their own, but they are not. Honestly, I probably wouldn't listen to me talk about those things either. I like stories, other people like stories, and I definitely have some stories that are unbelievable to say the least. Now that you know more about my journey with choosing positivity and coming to terms with the negative, its time to explore these concepts on your own.

WHAT STORIES DO YOU HAVE THAT ARE "UNBELIEVABLE"?

WHEN HAVE YOU CHOSEN POSITIVITY AND FELT EMPOWERED?

DO YOU THINK THAT WE NEED THE BAD TO UNDERSTAND GOOD?

ESSENTIAL OILS TO SUPPORT POSITIVITY AND RESILIENCE

- Stress Away™
- White Angelica™
- Surrender™
- Inspiration™
- Citrus Fresh™
- Orange
- Oola Grow™
- Into the Future™
- _____
- _____

SOCIAL MEDIA CHALLENGE

There is a lot of negativity on social media. Look to see what is trending on your favorite site and then create a post to emphasize what is good or positive about that topic. If you need examples of positive social media, don't forget to flip to Appendix B at the back of this guide!

CORE BELIEFS

Our minds are the key to success, but sometimes they can also be the reason we get stuck. Our past thoughts create our current reality, but there are many times that we create core beliefs that limit us from reaching our highest potential. It is important to explore our beliefs in order to better understand our challenges and our successes.

We are all shaped by our experiences and our environment and those things impact how we view the world and what we believe to be true about each other and ourselves. Many times we develop beliefs that keep us safe, sometimes we adopt the beliefs of the people who love and care for us, and we also have plenty of opportunities to create new beliefs based on our experiences. We often carry around beliefs that we don't even realize because they are a part of who we are and that is okay, unless those beliefs are holding us back.

In the last section, we talked about how positive is powerful and those positive, empowering beliefs are the ones we want to foster and leverage. Likewise, we want to uncover our negative, limiting beliefs so that we can work on creating a new story and ultimately a new reality.

What are some positive, empowering beliefs that you can foster? Basically, any beliefs that encourage, inspire, and empower you are a good place to start. Here are a few of my favorite ones that you can play around with to see how they feel when you say them.

"I am good enough."

"Every day is a good day."

"I deserve to be happy."

"I am worthy of having good people and nice things in my life."

"It is kind of fun to do the impossible." – Walt Disney

If these affirmations are overwhelming or trigger you, definitely spend more time with them and be sure to check out the Aroma Freedom Technique section.

ESSENTIAL OILS TO SUPPORT EMPOWERING BELIEFS

- Inner Child™
- Frankincense
- Release™
- Forgiveness™
- Believe™
- Transformation™
- Highest Potential™
- _____

SOCIAL MEDIA CHALLENGE

View some of your recent posts and see what kind of patterns you are creating in your mind. Based on the things you like to share, are you subconsciously looking for more things to hold you back, or to launch you toward your goals and dreams? Make sure you share at least one thing that is based on a positive belief that you have about yourself and/or the world.

#TeenOiler Testimonial
Sean Age 17

"The oils support my immune system during the long winter months when I don't have time to let myself be sidelined. They also provide a calming environment to get the rest I need to do my best in school."

WHAT DO YOU BELIEVE?

Belief is a pretty abstract concept, so I'm going to keep this part brief, but it is very difficult to promote a healthy mind without talking about the power of our beliefs. Since our thoughts become our beliefs, there is still an element of choice, but it isn't as easy or as obvious. Negative beliefs also hold us back more than negative thoughts because our beliefs guide our actions. So, the key here is to become a little more aware of the things that we believe to be true.

I'm pretty sure that I wouldn't know what to say if someone asked me what my core beliefs were when I was a teen, so I found two fun quizzes online for you to check out as a starting point. I don't want to influence your answers much more than this, so this part is going to really be up to you.

https://www.optimalthinking.com/personal-optimization/core-beliefs-quiz/

http://beliefworks.com/belief-quiz/

WHAT NEGATIVE BELIEFS DO YOU HAVE ABOUT YOURSELF OR THE WORLD THAT MIGHT BE HOLDING YOU BACK?

WHAT BELIEFS DO YOU HAVE ABOUT YOURSELF OR THE WORLD THAT MIGHT BE HELPING YOU TO REACH YOUR GOALS AND DREAMS?

Now, choose one negative or limiting belief and turn it around into something positive.

Write the positive thought down and focus on it while using your favorite essential oil at least twice daily.

Exploring beliefs is a challenging thing for most people, even adults. Please remember to be gentle with yourself, avoid judgment and keep an open mind. Since that is easier said than done, I want to introduce you to the concept of Mindfulness as a tool for slowing things down a little so we can get a good look at our thoughts and beliefs. Mindfulness has made a tremendous difference in my life and is now a huge part of all of my lessons and workshops.

What is Mindfulness?

Just like many of the other topics like essential oils, nutrition and exercise, this could be its own book and there are a TON of great books out there like *The Mindful Teen* by Dr. Dzung Vo, as well as some really cool apps like *Headspace*, that I highly recommend.

For our purposes, I'm going to paraphrase my favorite definition from one of the most well-known mindfulness masters, John Kabat-Zinn. He describes mindfulness as paying attention on purpose in the present moment without judgment. This is a very simplified definition but what he describes is definitely not simple in our fast-paced, multi-tasking culture of comparison also like to refer to mindfulness as "the fine art of chilling out" because it is important to set aside specific time to unplug, recharge, and do nothing. Although many people feel that doing nothing is a waste of time, it is actually important and very healthy for us. Mindfulness creates an opportunity to recharge and proves that we can control our thoughts and ultimately our actions.

Mindfulness is always described as a practice because it can be challenging to those of us who never slow down or pay attention on purpose, but the more we try, the easier it gets. If someone had told me a few years ago that I could actually slow my turbo-paced mind down and choose thoughts that were relaxing, I would've told them they were nuts. Luckily, no one told me that and I was introduced to this practice which has completely improved my life.

If you are ready to try mindfulness yourself, I highly recommend the *Headspace* app or, if you aren't tech-savvy, you can just begin by doing things differently so that they are more deliberate and require your full attention. Try eating or brushing your teeth with your left hand. Try to feel your heel and toes every time you take a step. Try to listen to only the music behind the lyrics in your favorite song. Try savoring your food for a few minutes before swallowing. Try anything that you normally try, but do it more slowly and more intentionally and make sure you don't judge yourself in the process.

My absolute favorite mindfulness practice is "Three Mindful Breaths" and, as simple as it might seem, it has had a massive impact on my mind. The reason so many of us get stressed out is that our minds end up spending too much time in the past or the future, so breathing helps us be present since it is impossible to breathe in the past or to breathe in the future. To practice "Three Mindful Breaths" on your own, start by closing your eyes and placing your hands on your abdomen. When you inhale slowly through your nose, you should feel your belly extend, and as you fully exhale out through your mouth, you should feel your belly button retract toward your spine. Repeat this process three times and then check in with your body to see how you feel.

Patty's Tips for being more Present and Mindful

- Slow down
- Pay attention to one thing at a time
- Avoid making judgments
- Use your physical senses (smell, taste, touch, hear, see)
- Unplug
- Make eye contact
- Don't worry about what other people are thinking
- Smile
- Breathe
- _____

ESSENTIAL OILS TO SUPPORT MINDFULNESS

- Present Time™
- Frankincense
- Oola Balance™
- Joy™
- Northern Lights Black Spruce™
- Purification™
- _____
- _____

SOCIAL MEDIA CHALLENGE

Be mindful of what you post. How will it make others feel? How does it make you feel? If it isn't uplifting for you and others, delete it.

Be mindful of what you follow on social media. How do the people and accounts you follow make you feel? Again, if it isn't uplifting, delete it.

MINDFULNESS REFLECTION

	WHAT DID YOU DO?	HOW DID YOU FEEL?
MINDFUL BREATHING		
MINDFUL LISTENING		
MINDFUL EATING		
MINDFUL WALKING		

Future Thoughts and Goals

I know we just explored and practiced mindfulness and being in the present moment, but it is also helpful to explore our minds by looking at some of our thoughts about the future. Being in the present moment is a great way to de-stress and connect with people, but we need to have a vision for where we are headed if we hope to achieve big things.

This isn't intended to overwhelm you and I'm not looking for a five-year plan complete with your college, grad school, house address, and baby names, but I am encouraging you to think about what you would like for yourself in a few key areas so that you can focus on those desires and make choices that move you in the right direction.

I believe we were all created for a unique purpose and that when we connect with that purpose, amazing things happen. So, for the next few sections, I really want you to dig deep into your reflections about the things you love and the ways in which you see yourself solving problems, helping others and making a difference. The more clarity we can get on our goals, the more we can use those goals to motivate us in a positive way today. Just like in the other sections, there is no right or wrong way to set goals. Some people get a lot out of SMART goals and that is something you can Google if you need some more help in this area, but my favorite goal setting approach is definitely the Oola Path and Oola Plan, so we will touch on those a little more when we discuss Oola.

Essential Oils to Support Goal Setting

- Into the Future™
- Stress Away™
- Build Your Dream™
- Oola Balance™
- Oola Grow™
- Oola Field™
- _____

SOCIAL MEDIA CHALLENGE

Find and follow at least one person who has a career you would love to learn more about. It can be a doctor, an athlete, an accountant, a gamer, or anything else you can imagine, but try to stay away from celebrities because the goal is for you to follow their posts to get insight into their everyday lives.

PATTY'S FAVORITE TOOLS FOR A HEALTHY MIND

There are so many healthy mind tools and I'm sure that as time goes on there will be apps for most of them. I've already shared a few of my go-to sources for mindfulness, so now I'm going to tell you a little about my favorite technique for emotional healing, and my favorite phenomenon for balance, goal-setting, and overall awesomeness.

OOLA

Oola is a term coined by the amazing Dr. Troy Amdahl and Dr. Dave Braun in their book, *Oola: Find Balance in an Unbalanced World*. Oola is a state of awesomeness where your life is balanced and growing and Young Living has helped turn Oola into a multi-sensory experience.

Dr. Troy is the "Oola Guru" and Dr. Dave is the "Oola Seeker" and together they tell their powerful stories of growth and transformation. Their book is super relatable and has clear action steps, plus the have an awesome online presence, they are super accessible, and you might even be able to catch them in person as they drive across the country in their Volkswagen Van covered in stickers and handwritten dreams.

You can check out the book and oil up with some Balance™, Grow™, or any of the oils for the seven key areas of life – Family, Friends, Faith, Fitness, Field, Finance, and Fun. Oola is for all ages, but having these tools at the beginning of your journey into life is a surefire way to prepare for greatness!

To get a little more Oola in your life, I want you to go to the website at www.oolalife.com and complete your Oola Wheel to see what areas of your life might be a little out of balance. Then I want you to take a minute to write down a goal for each area so you can get the most out of the book and the Oola Path and Oola Plan that you will learn about in the book.

FAMILY

FRIENDS

FAITH

FITNESS

FINANCE

FUN

FIELD (SCHOOL)

As you will learn from the Oola book, there are obstacles that make it harder to get to the Oola Life and the Oola guys call these obstacles "Oola Blockers". They are things like fear, anger, jealousy, self-sabotage, and laziness, and many of these blockers come from the limiting beliefs that we explored in the first part of this section. The stories we tell ourselves are incredibly powerful and also very believable because they are based on our experiences, so it sometimes takes a little extra help to turn the negative stories around or to get rid of them so empowering stories and beliefs can take their place.

Aroma Freedom Technique (AFT)

There are lots of great tools and techniques that help with mindset and limiting beliefs and I've experienced many of them from Neuro Linguistic Programming and the Emotional Freedom Technique (EFT) to Hypnosis and psychotherapy, but the easiest and most effective technique I've ever used to let go of limiting beliefs and bust through the mental barriers that were holding me back is Dr. Benjamin Perkus' Aroma Freedom Technique (AFT) with essential oils.

According to Dr. Perkus' website at www.aroma-freedom.myshopify.com, "The Aroma Freedom Technique quickly and easily releases you from negative thoughts, feelings, and memories so that you can achieve your dreams. Created by Dr. Benjamin Perkus, it integrates 20 years of Clinical Practice with 15 years of Essential Oil use. You can learn through Books, Trainings and Certification Programs."

I started with the book and ended up getting my certification because it was so transformative; I highly encourage you to find a practitioner or to learn the technique yourself if you have some emotional baggage that is holding you back, or just can't quite put your finger on what may be holding you back.

Go back to one of the goals that you made earlier and pick the one that seems the most challenging. Write it below and use it as Step 1 when you begin your AFT journey!

My Goal/Intention:

_____

My Affirmation (you'll create this after your session)

_____

WELLNESS FOR YOUR SPIRIT

I'm glad we just covered Oola because the affirmation for Oola Faith is "I am Humble, Grateful and Fully Connected." This is the perfect way for us to begin our exploration of spiritual wellness. I am not here to tell you what to believe about God or spirituality any more than I am here to tell you what to eat and who to hang out with, but we can't really cover wellness without talking about the importance of feeling fully connected.

For our exploration, I broke connection up into three different areas – connection to self, connection to others, and connection to something bigger, aka God. We are going to take a look at some of the heaviest topics in this guide including your feelings about yourself, your posse, and your God.

Our guidelines are especially important in this section, so please don't forget to keep an open mind and to take what works for you and leave the rest!

Mental and spiritual toxins aren't quite as easy to detect as the toxins that affect our bodies but they definitely stop us from experiencing wellness. These toxins can't be detected in a lab or scanned with a cool app on our phone, but they can cause just as much damage.

Judgment is a major toxin in this realm along with fear, envy, hatred, negativity, and anger (just to name a few). The good news is that we can learn to eliminate these toxins, but it is a process.

Patty's Tips for Spiritual Wellness

- Remember that this is process and there are many ways to connect with yourself, other people, and God
- Take time every single day to sit quietly and pray, meditate, and/or connect
- Practice gratitude every morning and every night before you go to bed
- Read books and follow blogs and pages that reinforce your beliefs
- Unplug to recharge
- Find someone you trust who shares your beliefs and ask them to mentor you
- Find other people your age who have similar beliefs and spend time with them
- Connect with people in real life
- _____
- _____

Essential Oils To Support Spiritual Wellness

- Sacred Frankincense™
- Frankincense
- Believe™
- Oola Faith™
- White Angelica™
- Exodus II™
- 3 Wise Men™
- Gratitude™
- Rose
- _____
- _____

Connection to Self

In the "You Matter" section, we briefly touched on the idea of self-love and I mentioned that it was not only the thing I wanted you to embrace the most, but it was also the most difficult. For some reason, there are a lot of conflicting messages about this kind of connection. Many of my students have told me that they can't focus on themselves or own their strengths because they don't want to be seen as self-centered and they don't want others to feel bad if they don't have similar strengths. Although I completely understand and empathize, I'm going to have you look at it in terms of a quote that changed my life -

> "Our deepest fear is not that we are inadequate. Our deepest fear is that we are powerful beyond measure. It is our light, not our darkness that most frightens us. We ask ourselves, 'Who am I to be brilliant, gorgeous, talented, fabulous?' Actually, who are you not to be? You are a child of God. Your playing small does not serve the world. There is nothing enlightened about shrinking so that other people won't feel insecure around you. We are all meant to shine, as children do. We were born to make manifest the glory of God that is within us. It's not just in some of us; it's in everyone. And as we let our own light shine, we unconsciously give other people permission to do the same. As we are liberated from our own fear, our presence automatically liberates others."
> — Marianne Williamson, *A Return to Love*

It can be a little scary or uncomfortable to fully focus on ourselves especially when we have a lot of limiting beliefs or when we fall into the trap of comparing ourselves to others, but Marianne Williamson's quote taught me how and why it is important to own our strengths, find our power, and shine our light.

PATTY'S TIPS FOR SELF-CONNECTION

- Remember that taking care of yourself and connecting with yourself is not selfish
- Be gentle with yourself
- Avoid comparison and judgment
- Focus on the positive
- If you can't let it go, let it be
- Treat yourself like you would treat your best friend
- _____
- _____

ESSENTIAL OILS TO SUPPORT INTRAPERSONAL CONNECTION

- Frankincense
- Inner Child™
- Joy™
- Oola Fun™
- Northern Lights Black Spruce™
- Grounding™
- Gratitude™
- _____

SOCIAL MEDIA CHALLENGE:

Unplug for at least 24 hours to recharge and reconnect with yourself. Notice your thoughts and feelings – especially if this is a huge challenge for you -- and implement as many of the tips from this section as you need to in order to be successful.

Connection to Others

In the last section, we discussed unplugging to recharge and connect with ourselves and I believe it is from that place that we can be our best selves and connect with others. However, most of us can't stay unplugged all the time. We live in the most technologically advanced, inter-connected society since the beginning of time, and this can be both a blessing and challenge. In an era when we can connect to other people at the click of a button, we are starting to lose touch with deep personal connections.

Group text chats, social media likes and comments, Snapchat Stories, and digital videos often connect us to friends and loved ones, but it is important to explore the depth of those connection and decide if they are strong enough to replace the bonds of personal interaction.

We've all witnessed groups of people, each on their own phone or other device, not interacting with each other in real life. Personal interactions, without electronics, provide a level of energy you seldom find online. There can be an almost palpable shared energy whether it's joy, laughter, stress, fear, whatever, that is meant to be shared. These energetic bonds are part of what makes us human and they are very difficult to convey through text and social media posts.

Although there are pros and cons to digital connection, the key to wellness in this regard is authenticity. If you are connecting with others in honest ways that reflect who you truly are and if you act with kindness and compassion, it doesn't really matter if you are online or in person - it is just getting harder and harder to connect in that way online with all of the distractions.

Patty's Tips for Connecting with Others

- Spend time with others in person
- Be yourself online
- Make eye contact
- Communicate your thoughts and feelings out loud
- Tell someone what you appreciate about them
- Be a good listener

- Celebrate the meaningful relationships in your life
- _____

ESSENTIAL OILS TO SUPPORT INTERPERSONAL CONNECTIONS

- Oola Friends™
- Oola Family™
- Gathering™
- Joy™
- Frankincense
- Acceptance™
- _____

SOCIAL MEDIA CHALLENGE

Find someone that you know and have met in real life but haven't talked to outside of social media in a long time and call them or ask them to hang out.

#SquadGoals –
An Honest Assessment of Your squad

"You are the average of the five people you spend the most time with" – Jim Rohn

I have a love/hate relationship with this quote… probably because I know it is true and my life is proof of its accuracy. I can directly attribute all of the happiness and success I have experienced to the people in my life (which is why my "Acknowledgements" page is actually two pages long), but I have also spent my fair share of time with people who have brought me down.

Make a list of the five people you spend the most time with and then write down their best and worst qualities.

Keep in mind, this exercise wasn't created to guilt trip you or to tell you who to hang out with, but it is one of the most important parts of this guide, so please take it seriously and really think about what you discover. If you find out that your posse is lifting you up and getting you to your goals – thank them! If you find out that the opposite is true, start brainstorming a way to distance yourself so you can get where you really want to go.

CONNECTION TO GOD

This part might be right up there with the Exercise section for me in regard to my level of experience and expertise, but I am a lot more comfortable writing about this thanks to amazing Young Living leaders like Gary & Mary Young, Monique McLean, Sarah Harnish, Adam Green, and the Oola Guys along with other faith-based leaders like Dr. Wayne Dyer, Mastin Kipp, Gabby Bernstein, Joel Osteen, Oprah Winfrey…

The Oola Guys actually inspired me to keep this as a section because I heard their story about keeping Oola Faith as part of their book just as I was starting to feel this connection in my own life and it left a big impression.

I wasn't raised in a particular religion and I will admit to being triggered by some friends and leaders as they referred to God in context with their happiness, their success, and their businesses. As a recovering control freak, it was hard for me to understand that there is a bigger picture and that we are all a part of it. Along the way, I've referred to that bigger picture as many different things – the Universe, Source, the Divine, Energy, the Force – and I've realized that we refer to it in infinite ways because of its infinite nature.

Personally, I had to have quite a few God experiences (formerly known as "coincidences") before I realized the power and importance of this connection. I now know experiences have nothing to do with age, so I hope you're coming to this section having already had your own connections. If you're not, don't worry – that is why this is here!

I know that discussing God, faith, and religion is a pretty big grey area in our society, but I also know that NOT discussing these things can cause people to suffer because they feel disconnected. If you are passionate about your beliefs and uncomfortable reading my thoughts on this topic, you're welcome to skip the next few pages, but I hope you'll stick around with an open mind and explore this aspect of your life a little more deeply.

I was 30 years old before I started feeling a spiritual connection and it completely transformed my life in every way. My faith gave me courage that I could barely fathom, it gave me words to give others hope, and it gave me a sense of purpose and belonging that I didn't even realize I had been looking for my whole life. Some of you may have been blessed with this connection since you were born and, if that is the case, I honor you and encourage you to hold on to that and share it when you can. You have a perfect opportunity to shine your light in a way that will inspire others to do the same!

Just like in the rest of the sections, I am going to tell you that it is my belief that there is no right or wrong way to connect with God as long as your intentions are good and you allow yourself to feel that connection. I am also going to remind you to avoid judgment and encourage you to keep an open mind so that you can love EVERYONE regardless of the details of their faith.

Judgment is the main toxin that stops people from having this connection, and I know that from personal experience. I was afraid to follow the wrong religion or to believe the wrong stories, or read the wrong scripture… so I read and studied all of the major religions along with a lot of non-denominational spirituality.

Through all that, I learned that that there is a dominant message in almost all religious teachings and that message is love and connection. When I realized that, I felt like my whole world opened up and that I could finally connect with God, as I understood Him.

My wish for you is that you always feel that connection and that you find it in a way that works for you, your family, and your values. If you struggle with this and don't feel connected, find a friend or relative who does and explore with them! So many churches in all denominations have youth programs and most of them would be happy to welcome someone new. At the very least, stay open to signs and "coincidences" so that you can have some tangible evidence that God is always there for you.

Essential Oils to Support Faith

- Oola Faith™
- Believe™
- Frankincense
- Sacred Frankincense™
- White Angelica™
- _____
- _____

Social Media Challenge

Find someone on social media who shares your religious beliefs, follow them, and share one of their posts that is meaningful to you. If you are Christian and haven't checked out Monique McLean and her 21 Days of Prayer, I highly recommend it!

Explore your beliefs and choose beliefs that make you feel good.

Write or draw what comes to your mind when you think about things that you believe to be true. I am definitely not going to tell you WHAT to believe, but I am encouraging you to think about what you DO believe because those things create your thoughts and ultimately the rest of your life.

This is a great topic to explore with a parent, teacher, friend, mentor, priest, minister, coach, or other trusted adult, but remember to make sure you are writing down YOUR beliefs and not what you think someone else wants you to believe because that will defeat the purpose.

Purpose

"When I was 5 years old, my mother always told me that happiness was the key to life. When I went to school, they asked me what I wanted to be when I grew up. I wrote down 'happy'. They told me I didn't understand the assignment, and I told them they didn't understand life." Attributed to John Lennon

There is some controversy over whether or not John Lennon said that or not, but the essence of the quote is still the key to this section. Some of you might think that you are too young to know what your purpose is and I know a LOT of adults who would struggle to answer this question. The goal here is not to stress you out, so if you feel yourself getting a little short of breath, go back to the stress management section and hang out there for a bit longer.

My goal here is to give you some alternatives to "What do you want to be when you grow up?" and to get you to start seeing your purpose as part of who you are - a part that doesn't necessarily change with age.

Instead of wracking your brain and thinking intellectually about your unique purpose, have some fun with this and start feeling how you want to feel - just like in the quote. What is something you could do all day every day and not get bored? What kind of things are you fascinated by? What makes you smile and lights up your day? All of these questions will get you closer to discovering your purpose.

Instead of thinking about what you want to be when you grow up, try these questions:

WHAT PROBLEMS DO YOU WANT TO SOLVE?

HOW DO YOU WANT TO FEEL?

WHO DO YOU WANT TO HELP?

HOW DO YOU WANT TO MAKE A DIFFERENCE?

Have fun with this and notice if any big ideas or patterns stick out for you because that is where you'll start to discover your purpose.

If this feels heavy and you need a pep talk, be sure to check out "A Pep Talk from Kid President to You" on YouTube!

ESSENTIAL OILS TO SUPPORT PURPOSE

- Oola Field™
- Frankincense
- Build Your Dream™
- Northern Lights Black Spruce™
- Valor™/Valor 2™
- Highest Potential™
- Acceptance™
- _____

SOCIAL MEDIA CHALLENGE

Create something that makes you feel good - something that makes you happy - and post it on your favorite site.

FINDING THE SWEET SPOT

Fill in the circle on the left with everything that you love. Fill in the circle on the right with all the ways you can make a difference. Then, look at both lists and see where they overlap – THAT is the sweet spot!

WHAT I LOVE   HOW I HELP OTHERS

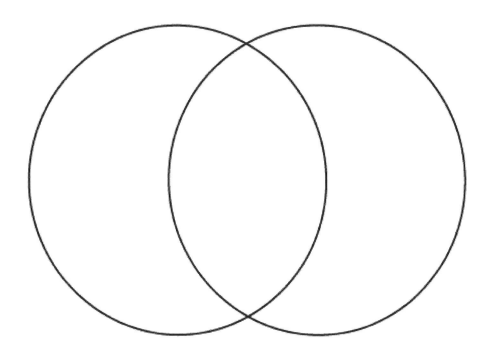

Pay it Forward

Once we are aware of our blessings, it is a lot of fun to share with others. "Pay it forward" just means you take what have and give some to another person in a gesture of kindness and gratitude. It works with really small things and really big things; there is no wrong way to pay things forward.

My first attempt at addressing teen wellness was a digital documentary, featuring my son and my students. I called it "Plan Be - Be Yourself, Be Awesome, Be the Change" because I wanted to encourage young people to BE instead of just telling them what to DO.

I created my Plan Be documentary because I know that young people are capable of incredible things. From volunteering at school, church, or in the community to committing random acts of kindness, caring for sick relatives, and inspiring the next generation, I have seen teens do so much to take their gifts and talents forward into the world. It was an honor to take the inspiration that my students always gave me and share it with the world like that, and I especially love hearing stories of how young people have taken my message and paid it forward to help others.

Essential Oils to Support Service to Others

- Gathering™
- Frankincense
- Stress Away™
- Live with Passion™
- Gratitude™
- Humility™
- _____

Social Media Challenge

Commit a Random Act of Kindness online. Post something thoughtful and tag a friend or loved one, boost someone up with your comments, share a post that will help others, make someone smile.

THE YOUNG LIVING FOUNDATION

One of my favorite ways to pay it forward is with the Young Living Foundation. I could fill another entire book with all of the amazing causes being championed by this remarkable organization, but this statement from the website really sums it up for me, "We believe empowerment is the key to long-term change."

Empowerment is at the heart of everything I do and is my biggest goal for you as a teen reading this guide. This quote and the following mission and vision statements can all be found on the Young Living Foundation website at www.younglivingfoundation.com.

Mission - The D. Gary Young, Young Living Foundation is committed to empowering individuals to achieve their potential and defy limitations by providing wellness and education opportunities to underserved communities.

Vision - We envision a world where children are provided with the resources and opportunities necessary to become confident, self-reliant leaders who can take control of their own health, provide for their families, and positively change their community.

You can visit the full site to learn everything you could possibly want to know about the Young Living Foundation, but there are two things that I want you to be aware of as you decide how to share your unique gifts with the world.

1. Integrity matters – Young Living covers all of the costs to run the Young Living foundation so that means 100% of all donations go directly to the cause! That is very rare in the non-profit world and makes such a huge difference.
2. It doesn't take a lot of money to make a massive impact. If every person who ordered from Young Living chose to round their order up to the closest dollar amount, that would mean almost $500,000 PER MONTH for these amazing causes! Did you know pocket change could make that much of a difference?!

Abundance

What is Abundance?

According to Dictionary.com, abundance is "an extremely plentiful or over-sufficient quantity or supply." Basically, when you have an abundance of something you have a LOT of something, generally more than you need. Abundance, as a concept, doesn't have a positive or negative focus, but many people connect the idea of abundance to the idea of money and material wealth. In that context, abundance can be a good thing, but there can also be an abundance of negative things like illness, poverty, and crime. So, for the sake of this section, we are going to practice one of our healthy mind tools and focus on what we want - the positive aspects of abundance.

What are some areas of your life where you would like to experience abundance? Love? Health? Wealth? Connection? Fame? Opportunities? Talent? Knowledge? Focus? Compassion? Creativity? Confidence? Enthusiasm? Optimism? Courage?

If the idea of abundance seems like a little too much for you because you prefer to share in equal opportunities with others, I honor your perspective but challenge you to look at abundance in some new ways, especially in terms of what it might mean for others. In my experience, having abundance has always been a way of blessing others, so if the thought of having more health, wealth, gifts, or opportunities makes you feel guilty, I encourage you to open up to that bigger picture. Once our needs are met and we have extra, we can use that extra to help others in amazing ways.

ABUNDANCE AS A MINDSET

There are many different types of abundance, but I want to highlight some of the ways that abundance ties into wellness and purpose, especially in terms of mindset.

Steven Covey explains the difference between a scarcity mindset and an abundant mindset when he writes, "People with a scarcity mentality tend to see everything in terms of win-lose. There is only so much; and if someone else has it, that means there will be less for me. The more principle-centered we become, the more we develop an abundance mentality, the more we are genuinely happy for the successes, well-being, achievements, recognition, and good fortune of other people. We believe their success adds to...rather than detracts from...our lives."

I believe that the abundance mentality described here is the key to creating your dream life and I did some reading and reflecting to come up with some ways we can develop our mindset in this direction. Basically, we need to follow many of the guides we have already discussed like focusing on what we want, taking care of ourselves, helping others, giving generously and spending time with others who have an abundance mindset.

WHAT KIND OF ABUNDANCE DO YOU WANT?

The awesome thing about this part is that not everyone wants the same things. Not the same kind of clothes or the same kind of car or even the same type of lifestyle will appeal to all people. If you find yourself questioning this because you interact with a lot of people who DO want the same clothes, shoes, cars, hairstyles, etc., I want you to take this activity very seriously. Sometimes it is difficult to know what WE want because we get caught up in what "everyone else" is doing and that is a dangerous place to be if you truly want to achieve wellness, purpose, and abundance.

This part may be easy for some of you who walk to the beat of your own drummer or those of you who know what you like and don't care what others think. For many of us, it is difficult and weird to think about our own needs and dreams separate from the people we want to impress and the people we care about the most in terms of love and acceptance. Just remember that this is YOUR book and it is also a No Judgment Zone. So allow yourself to think about what would make YOU the happiest and WHY it would make you happy. Having the latest clothes from an expensive store or having a new car might make you happy (things like that make many people happy), but when you start exploring the WHY, you'll get better insight about the choices that are best for you.

FINANCIAL ABUNDANCE

Let's face it, for many, if not most of us, when we think about wanting to have a lot of something, we think of money. So, our exploration of abundance wouldn't be complete without this subsection. I have made some pretty epic mistakes in this realm and I've definitely learned a LOT from all of that failure, and I am by no means a master in this area - yet! I definitely intend to master financial abundance and my plan is to learn from the leaders (both in and out of Young Living) who have figured out how to master the money game. Dave Ramsey is probably the most well-known financial guru and he has an entire teen series on his website. We also have our own Young Living version of Dave Ramsey - Steve Sheridan. His book *Journey to Health and Wealth* taught me so much about making better choices financially and he connects his lessons and information to the Young Living business model as well!

Patty's Top Tips for Abundance

- Be grateful for everything you already have
- Donate anything you don't need or use
- Keep track of your spending
- Avoid credit cards as much as possible
- Learn from people who are good at managing their money
- Save at least 10% of everything you earn
- _____
- _____

Essential Oils to Support Abundance

- Abundance™
- Gratitude™
- Frankincense
- Oola Grow™
- Surrender™
- Oola Finance™
- _____

Social Media Challenge

If you have social media, that means that you have more abundant resources than millions of others. Find and share an online cause like www.freerice.com and take action to share your abundance!

GRATITUDE

Did you know that it is impossible to feel stressed and blessed at the same time? It might sound crazy, but thoughts of stress and gratitude use different parts of our brain, so focusing on gratitude can relax that "fight or flight" feeling we get when we are stressed out about something.

The cool part about this is that our brains also like to look for patterns. As we spend more time focusing on the things that we are grateful for, we are naturally going to notice even more things to be grateful for and that will keep us feeling good.

Since I want to give my brain a little help to stay focused on gratitude, I have a practice of beginning and ending each day with gratitude. Each night, my husband, son, and I share our gratitude for something that happened that day. I encourage you to try something similar for a week and notice if anything changes.

PATTY'S TIPS FOR GRATITUDE:

- Each night, list or think about three things for which you're grateful
- Practice mindfulness -- pause a few times during the day and decide what you're grateful for at that moment
- Remember to be grateful for the challenges and obstacles from which you can learn and for the opportunities that present themselves before, during, and after the challenges
- _____
- _____

ESSENTIAL OILS TO SUPPORT GRATITUDE

- Gratitude™
- Abundance™
- Hope™
- Joy™
- _____

SOCIAL MEDIA CHALLENGE

Don't wait until November to express your gratitude! Commit to posting one thing you are grateful for each day on at least one platform. Use the hashtag #365grateful and see if you can make it an entire year!

GRATITUDE ACTIVITY

List five things for which you are grateful right now and say why you are grateful. Make sure you connect with the feelings and be as specific as possible.

1.

2.

3.

4.

5.

ACHIEVING ABUNDANCE WITH YOUNG LIVING'S BUSINESS OPPORTUNITY

Many teens feel limited by their employment opportunities – especially in small towns or in areas where there are a lot of teens competing for the same jobs. I wanted to include this section to let you know that there ARE awesome possibilities for teens as young as 16. You'll want to check with the person who shared this book with you to discuss this topic a little more fully, but you can start your very own Young Living Business as a teenager!*

I was actually inspired to include this section by a young man at last year's International Convention in Utah. I wish I had his name but I know I'll see him again one day because he has an incredible growth mindset and he knows his passion and purpose. He was only 15 years old, but he was attending the educational sessions at the Young Living convention because he knew he wanted to get in on the business opportunity in order to earn enough money to support himself while he pursued his dream of becoming an opera singer!

I realize that not many 15 year olds have that much of a plan and I definitely don't expect that by any means, but he reminded me of the power of possibility and showed me what happens when young people are given the right tools. I'm not saying that the Young Living business is going to be THE way for you, but it is A way. It also shows you that big things are possible for young people who take the time to explore their passions and their purpose, especially when they have a desire to help others. I now understand that network marketing and entrepreneurship are possibilities for anyone of ANY age, and that is so exciting!

Actually, there is a Young Living leader, Adam Green, who reached the highest rank, Royal Crown Diamond, by age 25 after only doing the business for a few short years! At this rank, he can earn a seven-figure salary and he did that with his passion for toxin-free living. If you're at all interested in this opportunity, you should definitely check out his book, *25 to Life* because he goes into detail about his journey and teaches you how to do it, too!

Some other awesome Young Living leaders have created resources that aren't as age-specific and I want to make sure you know about those as well because they illustrate the opportunity and the community you'll find with Young Living. Be sure to go to the "References and Resources at the end of this book for even more books, websites, YouTube Channels and more!

- Sarah Harnish - *Gameplan*
- Monique McLean - *Circle of Success*
- Steve Sheridan - *Journey to Health and Wealth*
- Andrew Jenkins – *The Field Guide to the Comp Plan*

The leadership and resources are amazing, but my favorite part of the Young Living business opportunity is the community. My whole team is like family to me. I love that I am part of a bigger network of "EntreprenOILers" and that we are all part of the whole Young Living movement. The Royal Crown Diamonds are so humble and connected and it is amazing to get knowledge, inspiration and training in so many different ways.

With Young Living, there are infinite opportunities for you to shine as an individual and share your unique abilities with others. The key ingredients for a successful Young Living business are all explained in detail in the *Gameplan* book, and I want to emphasize that it is an opportunity to grow in all three areas – wellness, purpose, and abundance. If you are consistent in your approach to a wellness lifestyle, your passion and joy will automatically connect you to others and those connections will enable you to develop lifelong connections as well as more creativity, compassion, confidence, and courage. As a former high school teacher and someone who works with teens for a living, I can't think of any better opportunity for developing those key skills. I also can't think of any other way that you can enhance those skills while earning money and helping people and the planet!

If this all seems like a little much, that is okay! Now you are aware that you have options in this realm just like you have with wellness and purpose! If any of this sounds interesting or exciting and you want to learn more, make sure you talk to the person who gave you this book so they can help.

#TeenOiler Testimonial
Emily Age 16

"Young Living has opened my eyes to the dangers that live in the world around me. There are so many horrible ingredients in different products I use daily, and after realizing this; our family has started to make drastic changes to our entire lifestyle. My parents started their oily journey around 2 years ago and I didn't really get into it until this year. My mom would say 'use this' or 'diffuse this' and I would just comply. Just recently, my parents surprised me with oils to help lift my spirits with oils for spiritual and emotional support. Since then, I have been using them like wild fire... I just can't get enough! I carry an entire arsenal of oils with me everywhere and wear a diffuser necklace to school daily. I have even shared oils with my friends at school too. I just became a Young Living member and paid for my own starter kit, so I can help others. This will also empower a continued education for myself about essential oils and show me how they can help me as a person. Since I made the decision to become an oiler, I have seen a difference in my lifestyle!"

* "To become a U.S. Young Living member, you must meet the following requirements:

• If you are an individual, be at least 18 years old

• An individual as young as 16 years old (a "Minor") may become a member upon the following conditions: The Minor's parent or guardian must sign the Member Agreement and agree to take full responsibility for the Minor member's account along with the Minor. The Minor will be required to operate the account using a unique form of payment for purchases on the member account (separate from the parent or guardian.) The Minor must also re-sign the Member Agreement when the Minor turns 18 years old. Failure to re-sign within three months of his/her 18th birthday may result in   a   hold   being   placed   on   the   Minor's   account."

Be the Change

Congratulations! You made it to the end of this guide, and that means you have explored wayyyyyy more about yourself, your choices, and your opportunities than most of the adults I know.

It could also mean that you're one of the people who skips to the end of the book, so if that is the case, I get it, but you'll have a lot more to work with if you go back to the beginning.

I guess the next logical question (if you are actually finished with the guide) is, "Now what?" and that is one of my favorite questions. We have already discussed the need for action throughout the entire book, so the metaphorical ball is now in your court.

What are you going to do now?

HOW ARE YOU GOING TO APPLY SOME OF THESE PRINCIPLES?

WHAT TOPICS DO YOU WANT TO EXPLORE AND LEARN MORE ABOUT?

WHO ARE YOU GOING TO HELP?

ARE YOU GOING TO KEEP SPREADING POSITIVITY ON SOCIAL MEDIA?

ARE YOU GOING TO KICK SOME TOXINS OUT OF YOUR LIFE?

ARE YOU READY TO USE ESSENTIAL OILS TO SUPPORT YOUR BODY, MIND, AND SPIRIT?

HOW ARE YOU GOING TO GET INVOLVED IN YOUR COMMUNITY?

I'm going to end this guide the same way I began it - by reminding you that **YOU MATTER**. As long as you commit to growing, work on staying positive, choose your thoughts carefully, and most importantly, take care of yourself, you will be the change we all so desperately need to see in the world, and I can't wait to watch that happen!

I can't wait to see where you go and I hope you keep me posted by tagging me in your stories of learning, growing, and adventuring.

Of course, our adventure wouldn't be complete without a few more thoughts from you, so take your time, enjoy the final reflection, and then create your wellness action plan so you can be your best self!

YOUR TOP 10 TAKEAWAYS FROM THIS BOOK

1.

2.

3.

4.

5.

6.

7.

8.

9.

10.

ACTION PLAN – CREATING NEW HABITS

Small actions and small changes, focused on regularly, can lead to big shifts so this final section is a place for you to commit to something small in each area. It can be from one of the tips, it can be to use a particular oil regularly, it can be to read some of the other books I've referenced throughout, but you should write at least one thing down that you can do to take action immediately.

WELLNESS

For my body, I will

_____

For my mind, I will

_____

For my spirit, I will

_____

PURPOSE

I will share my gifts and talents by

_____

ABUNDANCE

I will be more grateful about

_____

APPENDIX A:

The PDF version of the Young Living 2015 Worldwide Income Disclosure Statement can be found at –

https://static.youngliving.com/en-US/PDFS/incomedisclosurestatement_us.pdf

YOUNG LIVING 2015 WORLDWIDE INCOME DISCLOSURE STATEMENT

As a direct selling company selling essential oils, supplements, and other lifestyle products, Young Living offers opportunities for our members to build a business or simply receive discounts on our products.

Whatever your interest in the company, we hope to count you among the more than 1 million Young Living members joining us in our mission to bring Young Living essential oils to every home in the world.

What are my earning opportunities?

Members can earn commissions and bonuses as outlined in our Compensation Plan. As members move up in the ranks of Young Living, they become eligible for additional earning opportunities.

This document provides statistical, fiscal data about the average member income, average hours worked per week, and information about achieving various ranks

RANK	AVERAGE HOURS WORKED PER WEEK[3]	PERCENTAGE OF ALL MEMBERS[1]	MONTHLY INCOME[4]				ANNUALIZED AVERAGE INCOME[5]	MONTHS TO ACHIEVE THIS RANK[6]		
			Lowest	Highest	Median	Average		Low	Average	High
Distributor	3	90.1%	$0	$3,643	$0	$3	$17	N/A	N/A	N/A
Star	8	4.4%	$0	$834	$59	$79	$948	1	12	240
Senior Star	9	1.0%	$0	$1,089	$98	$226	$3,060	1	18	239
Executive	11	0.6%	$0	$12,404	$463	$549	$6,492	1	23	233
Silver	18	0.3%	$306	$27,826	$3,169	$2,271	$26,662	1	32	228
Gold	24	0.1%	$1,952	$39,655	$4,819	$6,042	$72,504	1	53	229
Platinum	33	< 0.1%	$5,084	$57,606	$12,043	$14,710	$176,520	2	63	238
Diamond	31	< 0.1%	$13,871	$144,369	$29,846	$38,750	$465,000	10	83	221
Crown Diamond	39	< 0.1%	$31,693	$208,597	$63,604	$74,325	$892,020	14	91	236
Royal Crown Diamond	37	< 0.1%	$53,723	$241,324	$144,985	$141,851	$1,702,212	17	126	230

The income statistics in this statement are for incomes earned7 by all active worldwide members in 2015. An "active" member is a member who has purchased at least 50 PV in the previous 12 months.8 The average annual income for all members in this time period was $28, and the median annual income for all members was $0. Forty-two percent of all members who enrolled in 2014 and 54 percent of all members who enrolled in 2013 did not remain active members with Young Living in 2015.

Please note that compensation paid to members summarized in this disclosure does not include expenses incurred by a member in the operation or promotion of his or her business, which can vary widely and might include advertising or promotional expenses, product samples, training, rent, telephone, internet, and miscellaneous expenses. The earnings of the members in this chart are not necessarily representative of the income, if any, that a Young Living member can or will earn through the Young Living Compensation Plan. These figures should not be considered as guarantees or projections of your actual earnings or profits. Your success will depend on individual diligence, work, effort, sales, skill, and market conditions. Young Living does not guarantee any income or rank success.

[1] Based on a count at the end of December 2015.
[2] Based on a survey of Young Living members in December 2015.
[3] Because a member's rank may change during the year, these percentages are not based on individual member rank throughout the entire year. They are based on the average distribution of member ranks during the entire year.
[4] Because a member's rank may change during the year, these incomes are not based on individual member incomes throughout the entire year. They are based on earnings of all members qualifying for each rank during any month throughout the year.
[5] This is calculated by multiplying the average monthly income by 12.
[6] These statistics include all historical ranking data for each rank and are not limited to members who achieved those ranks in 2015.

YOUNG LIVING
ESSENTIAL OILS

APPENDIX B:

10 SOCIAL MEDIA PROFILES THAT WILL CHANGE HOW YOU LOOK AT THE WORLD

The ten profiles listed below barely scratch the surface of what I discovered, but they are all incredibly powerful. Some are much more well-known than others, but each one is influential and unique, so I can definitely promise you and your loved ones a better social media experience if you choose to fill your feed with their posts and focus on their messages. At the very least, I urge you to check them out, ponder their posts, and share them with anyone who may be struggling with challenges related to the social and emotional aspects of social media.

A PLUS - POSITIVE JOURNALISM

According to their Facebook page, "A Plus is a digital media company co-founded by Ashton Kutcher that features stories that make a difference and create positive change."

As I mentioned in one of my most popular YouTube videos, we get more of what we look for online, so it is important to look for the good stories that showcase the positive side of humanity. Unfortunately, it often seems that the major media sources primarily cover stories of fear, destruction, and sadness – especially now, when political opinions are coming at us from every angle. Perhaps those stories sell better or someone is under the impression that people are looking for negativity and more reasons to worry, but for every story of despair, there are dozens filled with hope. Those stories are the ones highlighted by A Plus. Definitely follow A Plus on every platform if you would like to stay informed about our world while keeping your faith in humanity.

Born This Way - Empowering Youth, Inspiring Bravery

The company overview on Facebook says, "Led and directed by Lady Gaga and her mother Cynthia Germanotta, BTWF is committed to supporting the wellness of young people, and empowering them to create a kinder and braver world. We achieve this by shining a light on real people, quality research and authentic partnerships."

This description completely embodies the greatest needs of teens today. What more could we want for the next generation other than wellness, empowerment, and a kinder and braver world? Born this Way tackles tough issues in positive ways while providing great resources and a community of likeminded people who are supported by Lady Gaga and many other scholars and experts. Some of these experts have even come together to take a look at the emotional well being of teens throughout the country in order to start a much-needed "Emotion Revolution". Make sure to follow Born this Way to learn more about this important work and find out how you can help support and expand this crucial mission.

DoSomething.org - Any Cause, Anytime, Anywhere

The DoSomething.org website says, "We make the world suck less. One of the largest global orgs for young people and social change, our 5 million members in 130 countries tackle volunteer campaigns that impact every cause. Poverty. Discrimination. The environment. And everything else."

Adults, parents, and teachers often tell young people what not to do without giving them options about what they can and should do instead. This approach has led to rebellion and apathy among young people who want to help and make a difference in the world. Our young people are our greatest resource and their efforts are often tireless when they are connected to a worthwhile cause. DoSomething.org gives young people options and opportunities to use their voices and make a positive difference in the world. When kids are engaged in meaningful, relevant, and real-world opportunities, they are much less likely to make destructive decisions and they also increase their odds of future success. Check them out and follow their posts for inspiration and then make sure to go and do something!

ELLEN #BEKINDTOONEANOTHER

There isn't really a description or "about" section on Ellen's website because is safe to assume that most people know who she is and that they have been either directly or indirectly inspired or impacted by her at some point. Her humanitarian efforts and commitment to kindness make her social media channels a favorite of millions of people. She managed to break Twitter during the Oscars, she has her own video-hosting site, EllenTube, and she never fails to provide massive value with her content. Check her feeds every day to read stories of inspiration, empathy, and fun and don't forget to join her mission of encouraging everyone to be kind to one another.

EVERYONE MATTERS - EVERYONE IS IMPORTANT

"Everyone has the right to be who they are, without judgment, shame, attack or marginalization. We encourage acceptance of others and ourselves as we all are, and to thrive as our unique selves, with our own unique skills."

Everyone Matters launched in Fall 2012, and has attracted the support of global leaders, local governments, schools, businesses and organizations – along with the public – in collective advocacy of everyone's worth in society, everyone's right to dignity and respect, and for everyone's freedom to be who they are, without judgment. Along with organizations like the PTA, NAACP, Association of American People with Disabilities, Human Rights Campaign and the National Hispanic Media Coalition, many global figures have contributed affirmative statements of inclusion and empowerment. Archbishop Desmond Tutu, Sir Paul McCartney, Ellen DeGeneres, General Colin Powell, Hugh Jackman, Tom Brokaw, Kevin Spacey and others have all contributed along with many other everyday heroes of all ages, backgrounds, and cultures.

Aside from following the powerful posts, videos, and graphics shared by founder HeathCliff Rothman, you can also encourage your local schools, businesses, and politicians to get involved with activities, including the annual Everyone Matters Day which will be on April 12th this year!

JESSE LEWIS CHOOSE LOVE - 'NURTURING, HEALING, LOVE'

According to the website, "These three words have become the foundation of the Jesse Lewis Choose Love Movement and have evolved into a formula that is so simple, yet so profound that it has inspired people all over the world to not only choose love, but become part of the mission to help others do the same."

Through her book and social media platform, Scarlett Lewis tells the story of how she was able to find forgiveness in the midst of tremendous grief after losing her young son, Jesse, in the Sandy Hook Elementary School tragedy. This site is dedicated to promoting compassion, especially in schools, by urging everyone to "choose love". People of all ages can connect with this story and find inspiration to be more loving, so it is an awesome resource for helping our children understand unconditional love, empathy, and forgiveness. "Like" and follow Jesse Lewis Choose Love for inspiration, motivation, and concrete examples of love in action.

KID PRESIDENT (+ SOUL PANCAKE) - GIVE THE WORLD A REASON TO DANCE

"Brad Montague (writer, director) and Robby Novak (performer) are family. They make things together. They believe kids & grown ups can change the world."

If you haven't seen Kid President's "Pep Talk", please stop reading this right now, and go watch it. If you are already familiar with the viral video with the most adorable young man, then you know why he had to be on this list. Robby is one of the most inspirational and motivational people on the Internet and he appeals to students from Kindergarten through college (& beyond) because he is authentic, optimistic, funny, and, most of all, driven to make a difference. Brad and Robby continue to use their massive platform to highlight issues in a fun and meaningful way, and they always manage to keep smiling and dancing through it all. If the whole world could follow Kid President's leadership, the world would definitely be a much more "awesome" place.

I also have to mention Kid President's sponsor, Soul Pancake, because the rest of their content is pretty awesome as well. Their page says, "We provide some rockin' content (interviews, blogs, challenges, contests, features, and more), but it's really all about having YOU—the SoulPancake community—bring this site to life. Say what's on your mind. Be real. Talk about WHY WE'RE HERE." So, if you like to ponder big ideas and want to be part of the amazing community, definitely check out their pages as well!

CRAIG AND MARC KIELBURGER/WE DAY/FREE THE CHILDREN

Think "we" and act "we." Alone we may feel powerless, but together we can create a more peaceful, compassionate, and interconnected world.

According to FreetheChildren.com, "brothers Craig and Marc Kielburger are co-founders of our family of organizations leading social change: Free The Children, an international charity; ME to WE, an innovative social enterprise; and WE Day, a year-long educational initiative that culminates in a signature youth empowerment event."

We Day is a phenomenal event, and their page explains that, "[We Day] is an online community and an annual series of stadium-sized events that has brought together hundreds of thousands of youth to be inspired by the greatest leaders and entertainers of our time. Through We Act, young people turn inspiration into tangible results by learning about social issues and making a difference."

Between the various entities and the brothers who started it all, there is plenty of inspiration for anyone and everyone. So many young people feel that their thoughts and opinions are irrelevant, but this epic, international movement proves the opposite. Today's young people have powerful voices and they can make a huge difference – especially if they work together toward a shared vision of a better future. Check out their posts and pages to hear those voices and share the vision – together WE can make a difference.

OOLA - #LIVEOOLA

As their site explains, "Oola is simply a life that is balanced and growing in all the key areas of health and well-being. It can be a noun or a verb. It can be a destination or a feeling. It can be as complex as a life growing and balanced in fitness, finance family, field, faith, friends, and fun (the 7 F's of Oola), or as simple as a sunset, a quiet book on the beach, or a special moment with a child. It is that place we all shoot for in life. That feeling we experience and we celebrate our successes along the way. In short, Oola is cool."

Oola is really cool and so are the two guys who created the concept, Dr. Troy (aka The Oola Guru) and Dr. Dave (aka The Oola Seeker). Like Jesse Lewis Choose Love, this platform is also connected with a great book, but this time the book is for personal development. There are tons of great personal development platforms and many of them are listed on the results from my social media experiment, but this one made the list because it is new, fresh, and incredibly actionable – even for young people who might not be ready for the more intense volumes of personal development that we have grown to love over the years. Follow their posts to learn more about the Oola Dream Tour, to see and share great graphics and quotes, and to experience these inspirational guys first-hand through their daily Periscope broadcasts.

UPWORTHY - BECAUSE WE ARE ALL PART OF THE SAME STORY

"Upworthy draws massive amounts of attention to things that matter. Every day, we tell positive, genuine, meaningful stories that are worth reading, watching and sharing with your friends."

Posts from Upworthy have definitely taken over my feed in the past few months, and I am so grateful for their content and for their commitment to sharing things that matter. Many of their stories would count as positive journalism and they also share some stories that do not have a happy ending, but they do it in a way that is purposeful and compassionate. Perhaps the best part about Upworthy, especially for young people, is that they have a way of making important issues accessible and appealing for a broad audience. Definitely follow Upworthy on all platforms if you want to see more authentic and meaningful articles and experience the undeniable upside of easy-to-share content.

I hope that you have a chance to visit all of the sites and share their content with all of your fans and followers because the only way we can create a shift to more positive online experiences is to "be the change". Once you start liking, following, and sharing uplifting and meaningful posts, you will help them further their cause and you will also help introduce their content and ideas to all of your friends and family. Together we can definitely create a ripple effect of kindness, compassion, and creativity that will inspire and uplift people!

References and Resources

Books:

21 Days of Prayer for your Business by Monique McLean
25 to Life by Adam Green
Ancient Einkorn: Today's Staff of Life by D. Gary Young
Aroma Freedom Technnique by Dr. Benjamin Perkus
Circle of Success by Monique McLean
The Field Guide to the Comp Plan: Navigating Your Way to Abundance by Andrew Jenkins
French Aromatherapy: Essential Oil Recipes & Usage Guide by Jen O'Sullivan
Gameplan by Sarah Harnish
Journey to Health and Wealth by Steve Sheridan
The Mindful Teen by Dr. Dzung Vo
Oola: Find Balance in an Unbalanced World by Dr. Troy Amdahl and Dr. Dave Braun

YouTube Channels:

Adam Green @essentialHF
EntreprenOILers
Jen Springer @jenspringerchannel
Kid President @kidpresident
Lindsay Elmore @thefarmacistala
Monique McLean @lovethemcleans
YL Success Summit
Young Living @youngliving007

YouTube Videos:

"Body Evolution - Model Before and After"
"A Pep Talk from Kid President to You"
"Plan Be: Be Yourself. Be Awesome. Be the Change"
"Start with Why - Simon Sinek TEDTalk"

Apps

Headspace
irunurun
MyFitnessPal
Map My Run
TheEObar
THINK DIRTY

Websites

Aroma Freedom Technique - www.aroma-freedom.myshopify.com
Body Image Movement - www.bodyimagemovement.com
Environmental Working Group – www.ewg.org
Free Rice www.freerice.com
Lindsey Elmore PharmD – www.thefarmacistalabama.com
Living Green with Jen Springer – www.jenspringer.com
Monique McLean - www.lovethemcleans.com
Mindful.org - www.mindful.org
Mindful Teen – www.mindfulnessforteens.com
Oola - www.oolalife.com
Plan Be – www.planbethechange.com
Sarah Harnish/Oil Ability Team – www.oilabilityteam.com
Seed to Seal - www.seedtoseal.com
Sweet Savvy Minerals – www.sweetsavvyminerals.com
Young Living - www.youngliving.com
Young Living Business Monday Night Calls – www.oursimpletraining.com

ABOUT THE AUTHOR

Patty McLain is a Young Living Silver leader, certified secondary teacher, speaker, educational consultant, author, and youth wellness advocate. Patty earned her B.A. in English, teaching certificate, and M.S. in Education from Wilkes University where she also completed coursework in the Ed.D. program before taking time off to raise her son. Patty's wellness and empowerment practices are being used in schools around the globe as part of the Everyone Matters campaign where she has served as the School Programming and Student Empowerment Advisor since 2014. Through her work in schools, in the community, and privately, Patty has created a unique approach that focuses on creativity, compassion, confidence, positivity and mindfulness in order to equip teachers and students with enhanced personal, social, and emotional skills. Patty's Next Book, *Empowering Teens with Natural Wellness*, will be out later this spring.

To inquire about Youth Wellness Coaching, Group Workshops, or speaking engagements, visit www.thepattymclain.com.

Made in the USA
San Bernardino, CA
05 June 2017